PRIMA OFFICIAL GAME GUIDE

Written by Michael Knight

Product Manager: Jason Wigle

Senior Project Editor: Brooke N. Hall

Design and Layout: Calibre Grafix

Manufacturing: Stephanie Sanchez

Michael Knight has worked in the computer/video game industry since 1994 and has been an author with Prima Games for ten years, writing over 60 guides during this time. Michael has used both his degree in Military History and experience as a high school teacher to formulate and devise effective strategies and tactics for hit titles such as the Tom Clancy's Rainbow Six and Hitman series. He has also authored several titles in the *Star Wars* universe including *Star Wars* **Republic Commando**, *Star Wars* **Episode III:** *Revenge of the Sith*, *Star Wars* **Battlefront II**, and *Star Wars:* **Empire at War**. Michael has also developed scenarios/missions and written game manuals for SSI, Red Storm Entertainment, and Novalogic.

When he is not busy at work on an upcoming strategy guide, Michael likes to spend time with his wife and four children at their home in Northern California. It was with their help that Michael used his abilities and experience to write three travel/strategy guides on Disneyland and Southern California, in which he developed tips and hints to help vacationing families save time and money while maximizing their fun.

We want to hear from you! E-mail comments and feedback to mknight@primagames.com.

ISBN: 978-0-7615-5640-4

Library of Congress Catalog Card Number: 2007922910

Printed in the United States of America

07 08 09 10 LL 10 9 8 7 6 5 4 3 2 1

PRIMA GAMES
A Division of Random House, Inc.
3000 Lava Ridge Court, Suite 100
Roseville, CA 95661
www.primagames.com

# Contents

# Training and Tactics

The year is 2014, and Captain Scott Mitchell and his Ghost Squad have completed their assignment in Mexico City, where elements of the Mexican military tried to take over the government. However, upon returning to the United States, Mitchell must get ready to go back into action. The conflict between the Mexican loyalists and the insurgent rebels has erupted into a full-scale civil war that threatens to spread its violence and destruction north into the U.S.

This is *Tom Clancy's Ghost Recon: Advanced Warfighter 2*. It continues where its predecessor left off. Once again you take the role of Scott Mitchell as the commander of the Ghost Squad. You will be operating across the border in Mexico as well as within the United States. This guide contains all the information necessary to succeed in the game; this chapter covers the basics of the game as well as the tactics you need on a modern battlefield. There are some new features in *Ghost Recon Advanced Warfighter 2*, so be sure to review this chapter even if you are a veteran of the first game. Subsequent chapters cover the members of the Ghost Squad, the weapons in the game, a complete and detailed walkthrough of the single-player campaign, and finally strategy, tips, and maps for the multiplayer game. Gamer achievements for the Xbox 360 version of the game can be found at the end of the guide. So before you strap on your equipment and load your weapons, take some time to prepare for the combat ahead.

# Fundamentals of Tactical Combat

Let's take a look at some of the basics you need to know to survive out on the battlefields of the 21st century.

## SITUATIONAL AWARENESS TACTICAL DISPLAY

Your display contains a lot of information for use during combat.

One of the most important factors on the battlefield is situational awareness. This term means the ability to know what is going on around you, even while in the chaos of combat. Commanders who know where their troops are as well as the position and composition of the enemy can make better decisions on how to operate and use their forces more effectively. The situational awareness tactical display is at the core of the advanced warfighter system. With this, you can identify threats first and make quicker, more accurate tactical decisions. This display is the game screen. In your role as Captain Mitchell, you are the center or hub of what is called the Cross-Com system. On your heads-up display (HUD), all information received from your assets is shown. The locations of detected hostiles, both infantry and vehicles—whether you can personally see them or not—will be shown via red "intel" markers. Objectives are designated by yellow square markers, while the locations of friendlies are shown with green or blue markers.

# MOVEMENT

You have to get around the battlefield primarily on foot.

Moving your character is accomplished with the two analog sticks. Use the left analog stick to move forward, backward, and strafe to the left or right. This stick also controls speed—gently pushing the stick forward causes you to walk, while pushing the stick completely forward makes you run. The right analog stick controls where you're looking or aiming—up, down, left, or right. If you're new to this sort of game, getting used to the controls can take some practice. But after a few minutes of gameplay, you'll get the hang of it.

# STANCE

Your fire is more accurate when you lie prone.

Your character can assume three different stances. Standing allows for the quickest movement and decent weapon accuracy. Crouching reduces speed considerably but constricts the weapon's aiming reticle, indicating a more stable shooting stance and greater accuracy. Stealth is also increased when you crouch, allowing you to more easily evade detection, even if you're not hiding behind an object. The third stance is prone. Crawling in the prone position is the slowest form of movement, but it's also the most stable shooting stance, capable of enhancing the accuracy of any weapon. Light machine guns and sniper rifles benefit greatly from the prone stance, which allows the shooter to better manage the weapon's weight and intense recoil. While prone, you can roll laterally. This is useful for quickly moving in and out of cover without switching stances. For example, try rolling around a corner to engage hostiles and then rolling back behind cover to reload.

# COVER

Take cover behind walls and other objects for protection.

During combat, the object is to kill the enemy while avoiding getting killed yourself. You need to keep something between you and the enemy. If that something prevents the enemy from seeing you, such as smoke or camouflage, it is referred to as concealment. However, you also want something between you and the enemy that will stop a bullet. You need cover. Surviving combat relies heavily on your ability to utilize cover. The enemy is very accurate, and staying out in the open during a firefight is a sure way to be hit. Using cover is very easy. Simply put a sturdy object between yourself and the incoming bullets. Move your character to the source of cover, such as a wall or vehicle, and continue to press against the object to have your character automatically take cover behind it. Once behind cover, you can peek around it to spot and engage hostiles. To do this, move along the object to the corner and peek around the side. You exit cover mode by pulling away from the object or pressing the action button. Be careful when choosing an object to hide behind, as all forms of cover are not equal. For best results, seek out objects constructed from heavy materials like steel, stone, or concrete.

# ENVG

**Warm bodies stand out in the dark when you use ENVG.**

Sometimes you operate in low light and/or low-visibility situations. There is nothing to worry about. Your equipment includes enhanced night-vision goggles or ENVG. In the past you had either night-vision or thermal-imaging goggles. However, ENVG combines the two into a single display. The night-vision ability allows you to see your environment in the dark, while the thermal-imaging ability makes warm objects, such as bodies and operating vehicles, stand out from the cooler surroundings. ENVG can also be used to see enemy targets through smoke. However, be careful when using this feature during daylight operations since bright light tends to blind your view, making everything look white.

# Weapons

As the premier Special Forces unit, the Ghosts have a variety of weapons at their disposal, each capable of inflicting serious damage. Let's take a quick look at the different types.

## FIREARMS

Use the scope view when targeting distant hostiles. Hold your breath for greater accuracy.

Although each firearm in the Ghosts' arsenal has unique characteristics, they all function similarly. Simply center a target in the aiming reticle on the HUD and squeeze the trigger. The aiming reticle shows where your bullets are likely to hit. This circle constricts and expands based on movement, stance, and weapon recoil. For example, the circle expands to its largest size when you're running while firing an automatic weapon. It shrinks to its

smallest size when you're stationary and prone. As a result, your weapon is most accurate when fired from a stationary and stable stance.

## TIP

For greater accuracy at medium range, hold down ⓛ to enter precision aiming mode.

Most firearms have different firing modes governing how many rounds are fired with each trigger pull. These modes include fully automatic, semi-automatic, and burst. To conserve ammo and reduce the effects of recoil, consider operating your weapons in semi-automatic or burst mode. If automatic is the only setting available, fire in short bursts to keep the weapon on target. Monitor the expansion of the aiming reticle while firing. As it grows, lay off the trigger and wait for it to shrink before firing another burst.

## TIP

Most assault rifles and all sniper rifles have scopes. To switch to scope view, click the right analog stick. Clicking again cycles through increased magnification if available and then returns to standard view. When peering through a weapon's scope, hold your breath (hold down ⓛ) to steady your aim, and always go for head shots to guarantee a kill.

# Explosives

**Satchel charges or C4 can be used to destroy vehicles when a bit more firepower than that of a grenade is needed.**

The Ghosts have access to two types of explosives: fragmentation grenades and satchel charges. Frag grenades can be thrown at varying distances based on the amount of time the fire button or trigger is depressed. For a long throw, hold down the fire button for a few seconds, then release. Make a short toss by tapping the button—just make sure you're behind cover when using grenades in close-range engagements. The grenade will not be thrown until the fire button is released, nor will it explode in your hand. It's equipped with a four- to five-second fuse, which is activated when the grenade is thrown, allowing it to bounce and roll around. Grenades are most effective against infantry but can also damage vehicles. Try tossing them beneath vehicles to maximize the damage. If you throw the grenade directly at a vehicle, it will probably bounce off, landing several feet away from the target.

Satchel charges have a lot more explosive firepower than grenades, and they are capable of taking out any vehicle. They can be thrown like grenades, but because of their heavier weight, they won't travel as far. Once thrown, the satchel charge must be detonated by remote control. You automatically switch to the remote detonator. You must be looking in the direction of the satchel charge to detonate it.

C4 is a more specialized explosive, used primarily to destroy enemy equipment and vehicles. In most cases, the deployment of C4 is associated with the demolition of a specific objective. You can't choose to take C4 with you on a mission. It is automatically included and can be placed only on objectives. C4 charges are equipped with a timer that is set automatically when the explosive is stuck to an object. As the timer ticks down, run away and seek cover before the charge detonates.

# FIXED WEAPONS

The mini-gun on the Blackhawk can put out a lot of lead in a short amount of time.

Sometimes standard hand-held firearms aren't enough to hold back the enemy. In such instances, get familiar with fixed weapons such as the fixed machine gun and the Blackhawk-mounted mini-gun. Fixed M50 machine guns can be found on the battlefield in some single-player campaign missions. These guns are often manned by hostiles, but you can use them. You also make several gun runs in the Blackhawk using the door-mounted M134 mini-gun. This rapid-firing behemoth uses rotating barrels to unleash a barrage of automatic fire. It takes a second or two for the barrels to begin spinning, so prepare for a slight warm-up delay after pulling the trigger.

These fixed weapons are much more stable than their hand-held counterparts, capable of accurate, sustained fire. They also have unlimited ammo. However, they have a tendency to overheat, leading to misfires and complete malfunction. Watch the weapon's heat meter in the bottom-right corner of the screen, and fire in short bursts to keep the temperature low.

## TIP

Teammates can use the fixed-machine-gun positions. Order them to move to a position and one of your Ghosts will man the gun. When possible, put a team member behind a machine gun while you provide support with a sniper rifle or move to a flanking position.

# The Cross-Com

The Cross-Com in the upper-left corner lets you give orders to your support assets.

As Captain Mitchell, the Ghost leader, you have access to a variety of military support elements, all accessible through the Cross-Com. This communications system links you to your team and all surrounding elements. Targeting information is shared instantaneously among all connected elements in the form of intel markers—red diamond icons that appear on your HUD and tactical map. Each unit in the Cross-Com network is informed of all known intel, whether individual line of sight is established or not. This powerful system is extremely useful, especially when its capabilities are fully exploited.

The Cross-Com window is in the upper-left corner of the HUD. This window shows the currently selected support element and a camera view from the asset's perspective. You cycle through the available support elements by pressing left and right on the D-pad.

## COMMAND FULL VIEW

See what your support assets can see on the battlefield from their point of view.

One of the features new to *Ghost Recon: Advanced Warfighter 2* is the command full view or CFV. To activate this feature, hold down ⓛⓑ. (You can change this command to a toggle feature so you don't have to hold down ⓛⓑ by changing the setting in the General Options screen.) The screen view changes so you see what the currently selected unit on your Cross-Com sees. Within the CFV, you have control of a camera, which you can rotate around to get a good view of the surroundings of the selected support. Press the left analog stick to change the view to another member of your team or the right analog stick to center the view back to its default.

### TIP

Use the reticle in the center of the screen just like you would your own reticle for giving orders to the selected support. The CFV can be used for all of your support assets—not just the Ghost Squad.

# Battlefield Support

There are various types of support available to you. Over some you have direct control, while others are more limited.

## GHOST SQUAD

The Ghosts help you complete your objectives during most missions.

The Ghost Squad is composed of three of your teammates and is your primary support for most missions. Once selected in the Cross-Com, the Ghost Squad can be ordered to go to a selected position when you press up on the D-pad or to regroup on you when you press down on the D-pad. When ordering the squad to move to a location, simply aim your reticle where you want it to move, then press up on the D-pad. Try to order your team to move behind some piece of cover. In urban settings, make frequent use of building corners—the squad will automatically assume a cover position and peek around the corner to scan for hostiles.

You can also order your team to attack a specific target. Simply center your reticle over an intel marker for a hostile and press up on the D-pad. Your team will then try to engage the enemy.

You control the aggressiveness of the squad by changing its rules of engagement (ROE). The default ROE setting is Recon. In this mode your teammates report the presence of hostile units and fire only if fired upon. Assault mode allows the squad to engage all hostiles on contact. This is useful when attacking or defending. For the most part, keep the ROE set to Recon to stealthily gather all intel before directing follow-up actions.

At times you may want to give your team, or another element of support, orders at a distance. This can make it difficult to use your reticle. Instead, open up the tactical map. Adjust the map so you have a direct, overhead view. Then move the small reticle in the center of the map over a location to move to or an enemy to attack and give the appropriate command with the Cross-Com.

# UAV 3

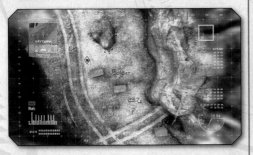

Use the UAV to detect hostiles.

During some missions, you have an unmanned aerial vehicle tasked to you. The UAV is used for reconnaissance and allows you to detect enemy units without exposing you or your team. Give it movement orders using the Cross-Com and it will fly at high altitude to the designated location. However, to detect hostiles, you must fly it at low altitude. To do this, switch to CFV and then fly it around using the two analog sticks. As you fly over hostiles, red intel markers appear. When the UAV is at low altitude, enemies can see and fire on it, so don't stay low over them. Instead, exit CFV to return the UAV to a safe higher altitude. While it can't detect new hostiles at high altitude, it will continue to monitor detected enemies as long as they stay within the UAV's monitoring radius. This allows you to follow enemy movements. If you have a UAV tasked to you, be sure to use it to scout out an area before you move in.

# MULE

The MULE is a mobile resupply drone.

Another new addition to the game is the MULE. This land drone carries equipment around the battlefield. Access its rear hatch to resupply your ammo or switch weapons. You can give movement orders to the MULE through the Cross-Com or take direct control of it through the CFV, where you can actually drive it around the battlefield.

# GROUND SUPPORT

A Stryker can give your team a lot of extra firepower.

Ground support consists of vehicles over which you are given some control, such as a Stryker armored vehicle. Ground support vehicles can only travel along a set route, so your movement orders are limited to move forward, move back, and stop. You can also give them attack orders and access them through the CFV. These ground support units can provide you with a lot of additional firepower. Just be sure the enemy does not have any anti-tank capability or heavy weapons that might destroy the vehicle. You can use ground support as mobile cover when advancing on the enemy.

# AIR SUPPORT

Call in an air strike against tanks.

Air support consists of air units such as AH-64 Apache gunships and F-15 fighter-bombers. Your control of air support is limited to designating a target for it to attack. The units are usually tasked to you when you run into enemy tanks and need some additional firepower. Select targets with the reticle on your HUD or on the tactical map.

# Rally Points

Select your team at a rally point.

Rally points are available in some missions. They consist either of a Ghost truck or a Blackhawk. Moving to these objectives allows you to change teammates and weapons. There are six different classes of teammates, but not every type is represented at each rally point. Each class carries a specific type of weapon:

- Rifleman: Each rifleman carries a scope-equipped assault rifle; this teammate is good for short- to midrange infantry engagements.
- Grenadier: The grenadier's assault rifle/grenade launcher combo is useful when you face a variety of threats, including lightly armored vehicles.
- Gunner: Equipped with light machine guns, the gunners can lay down heavy suppressing fire but lack the precision of the other classes.
- Marksman: This is your sniper. Their high-powered rifles are great for long-range kills but practically worthless in firefights.
- Anti-Tank Gunner: The anti-tank gunner carries the Zeus MPAR, a vital weapon system used to destroy heavily armored vehicles such as APCs and tanks.
- Combat Medic: The combat medic is armed with a submachine gun and comes with more medikits than other classes. This soldier can heal other soldiers better and is the only one who can heal you.

Choose your three team members carefully, as each choice impacts the offensive capabilities of your squad. Rally points also allow you to choose a primary weapon, a secondary weapon, and a grenade pack. When possible, choose a weapon that complements your team's firepower. For instance, if you don't have a grenadier, choose a weapon with a grenade launcher. After you visit a rally point, any personal injuries sustained during combat are healed.

# Advanced Tactics

The single-player campaigns require a heightened sense of awareness and tactical know-how to make it through unscathed. Now that you have a firm understanding of the basics, let's go over a few advanced tips and tactics to help you get started.

## COVER ASSESSMENT

When in a firefight, make sure you are behind something solid, like a concrete wall or planter.

Choose your cover carefully. Cars can be found in some areas, but they don't offer the best cover because of the large window openings. Instead, seek out solid steel and concrete objects. Low walls are decent as long as you stay crouched behind them. Instead of standing up and firing over low pieces of cover, remain crouched and fire around them to maintain a low visible profile and greater weapon accuracy.

## CORNER POSITIONS

Order your team to move to the corners of buildings to get a view of what is on the other side.

Always use corner positions to scout ahead. Peek around corners before walking out into a new area—crouch down before peeking to minimize your exposure. Team members perform the same action when moved to a corner. Assuming the ROE is set to Recon and they're not spotted, they'll report back, updating your HUD and tactical map with fresh intel.

# SMOKE FOR CONCEALMENT

Smoke conceals your location and allows you to move across open areas undetected.

Smoke grenades are included in the offensive and defensive grenade packs. Although they're great for concealing movement, they can also be used offensively when combined with your ENVG. Toss a smoke grenade in front of an enemy position and wait for the smoke screen to form. Then, activate your ENVG. Enemies can't see through the smoke, so they won't fire at you. But the thermal-imaging optics allow you to see their heat signatures. Steady your aim and fire before your smoke screen thins out.

# FIX AND FLANK

When enemies hide behind cover, hit them from the side or rear.

The enemy AI responds realistically to coming under fire by seeking cover. While behind cover, hostiles peek out occasionally and take shots at you and your team. Eliminating enemies behind cover can be difficult if they're well concealed. Your best option is to flank them from a different angle. Start by firing on the covered hostiles to keep their heads down. Meanwhile, order your team to a flanking position. It's important to keep the enemy pinned with suppressing fire until your team is safely behind cover. As your team gets closer, the enemy may freak out and attempt to flee, inadvertently stepping into your line of fire. If the enemy stays put, move to a different flanking position while your team suppresses. Continue moving and suppressing until the enemy is dead, or until you're within hand-grenade range.

# VEHICLE ENGAGEMENTS

Enemy vehicles pose a serious threat to your team and support assets. When possible, call in heavy support to eliminate them. However, sometimes you have no choice but to deal with them on your own. Following are some tips on destroying the various enemy vehicles you encounter during the campaign.

## LIGHTLY SKINNED VEHICLES

Try using satchel charges placed in the road to destroy enemy vehicles as they drive over the charges.

Both troop trucks and Panhards can be destroyed with small-arms fire, but it takes several seconds of intense team fire before they go up in flames. Grenades (either tossed or launched) and light machine guns can speed up the process. Try to destroy trucks before they can come to a stop and unload their reinforcements. Panhards can be neutralized (but not destroyed) by picking off the machine gunner on the vehicle's top-mounted turret.

## LIGHT AND HEAVY ARMOR

## HELICOPTERS

Rocket launchers such as the Zeus T2 work great against armored vehicles. You can destroy APCs with a single hit, but tanks take two hits.

Destroying APCs, artillery units, and tanks requires heavier weapons, as their thick armored hulls are resistant to small-arms fire. The Mowag APCs used by rebel forces can be damaged and even destroyed by consecutive hits from grenade launchers and the Blackhawk's mini-gun. Still, avoid toe-to-toe engagements with these vehicles—their weapons can chew up your squad in record time. When it comes to taking out tanks, you need the Zeus T2, Zeus MPAR, or support from friendly armor and air units. Self-propelled artillery and anti-aircraft units pose no immediate threat to you or your team, but they're usually well guarded. Destroy them with C4 charges.

Helicopters can be a big threat to your team. Shoot them down as quickly as possible.

Attack and transport helicopters are another serious threat that must be dealt with quickly. The best way to take them out is with a light machine gun—or a fixed machine gun if one is nearby. The high rates of fire of these weapons are good for hitting these moving targets. In a pinch, Zeus T2 and Zeus MPAR rockets can also cause heavy damage—if you can score a hit.

### TIP

You can also use satchel charges to take out armored units.

# The Ghosts

# Captain Scott Mitchell

## STATS

**DOB:** 08/13/76

**Age:** 37

**Rank:** Captain

**Service:** U.S. Army, 7th SFG

**Position:** Ghost Team Leader

## PERSONAL

Scott Mitchell was born and raised in Youngstown, Ohio. His father was a factory worker who took pride in the fact that he worked his way up to foreman. His mother, who emigrated from Latvia at age 10, was an assistant pharmacist. She passed away when Mitchell was 14.

Mitchell is the oldest of four children, with two brothers and a sister. With both parents working, Mitchell grew up independent and self-reliant. After his mother's death, he also took on the responsibility of helping to raise his younger siblings, which instilled in him a strong sense of leadership. He was an above-average student and worked part-time as a shop assistant for an automobile mechanic.

After graduating from high school, Mitchell found that he could not afford to attend college. He chose to go into the military, joining the Army instead. Initially, his plan was to serve and then go to school using G.I. Bill benefits, but he found the Army lifestyle suited him, and he became a professional soldier.

## MILITARY

Mitchell attended basic training at Fort Drum. His high scores on linguistics screening made him eligible for entry into counterintelligence, but he declined and entered the infantry. His initial service was at various stations, including peacekeeping tours in Bosnia and Kosovo. During this time he earned the Army Commendation Medal.

After a few years of infantry service, Sergeant Mitchell attended Airborne training at Fort Benning. Shortly thereafter he was assigned to OPFOR and spent the next two years working as a team leader for an OPFOR recon unit at Fort Irwin. While serving in OPFOR, Staff Sergeant Mitchell completed his B.A. in history through night school and correspondence.

During his time at OPFOR, Staff Sergeant Mitchell applied for and received transfer to Special Forces. Soon after completing Special Forces training at Fort Bragg, he applied for and received his commission. His first Special Forces assignment was the Philippines, where he served as one of the members of the 12-man "A-Teams" that deployed to train Filipino troops in their campaign against the Abu Sayyaf. First Lieutenant Mitchell earned a Silver Star for action against guerilla units when his team was ambushed while on a patrol on Basilan.

First Lieutenant Mitchell returned to the U.S. after his service in the Philippines and was recruited by the Ghosts just in time for deployment to Georgia. He went on to serve in Eritrea and Cuba, where he earned the Silver Star and was promoted to captain. At this time, he also took a team leader position within the Ghosts. Recently, Captain Mitchell was slated for promotion to major but delayed his promotion in order to stay with the Ghosts for their deployment to Asia. Since returning he has been promoted to major.

## DEMEANOR

Scott Mitchell is a professional soldier. He believes that whatever job one does, one should do it to the best of one's abilities, and he applies that philosophy to soldiering.

As a leader, Mitchell leads by example and believes that respect is earned. He knows that his troops are the very best and treats them like the professionals they are. In a military setting, he is a no-nonsense soldier. He puts the mission and his team first, and everything else is secondary. In the field, he leads by example and projects a calm and professional demeanor to his troops. He is apolitical and doesn't concern himself with the politics of the missions.

In addition to English, Mitchell speaks fluent Spanish and passable French.

## OFF DUTY

Off duty, Scott Mitchell has a small apartment at the Fort Bragg BOQ. He has a passion for carpentry and enjoys building furniture that he sells to other soldiers on base. He rents a storage garage where he keeps his small woodshop. On longer leaves he travels home to visit his family, which still resides in Ohio.

# Jose Ramirez—Rifleman

## STATS

**DOB:** 12/12/78

**Age:** 35

**Rank:** Sergeant

**Service:** U.S. Army, 7th SFG

**Duties:** Rifleman, Communications

## MILITARY

Entering the U.S. Army was a shock to the young introverted Jose. The Army was unlike anything he'd ever experienced. After a rough boot camp, Jose's gunny realized that this undisciplined youth had an iron will, and was smart to boot. A short talk with Jose, now "Joe," convinced the young soldier to apply for Ranger School.

Joe came away from two tours in the Pashtun region of Pakistan with a Purple Heart and a Silver Star. A career soldier who preferred being in the field to being behind a desk, he turned down an office job at OCS for a role in the recently formed Ghosts.

Joe is new to OPFOR, but he's quick on the uptake and knows his job.

## DEMEANOR

Joe is a funny guy that everybody loves, always keen on cracking jokes. The conflict in Mexico touches him personally, as he still has strong family links there.

## PERSONAL

Jose Ramirez is a first-generation Mexican American born in the suburbs of Los Angeles, California. Jose never found common ground with his parents, who stuck tightly to the traditions of the life they'd left behind in Mexico. His need to be alone led him to pursue his true passion: radios. A ham radio operator from the time he was 10, Jose enjoyed creating links that spanned the world. The explosion of the Internet in the late '90s only increased his desire to learn about faraway people and places. His connections grew, his skills increased.

After graduating from high school Jose drifted into the hacker community. After a few brushes with the law, a police officer suggested that he go into the Army and settle down before he did something really stupid.

# Paul Smith—Rifleman

## STATS

**DOB:** 04/19/88

**Age:** 25

**Rank:** Sergeant

**Service:** U.S. Army, 7th SFG

**Duties:** Rifleman

## PERSONAL

Paul was raised in the backwoods of California's Modoc County, where his father was the local sheriff. An avid outdoorsman, Paul's father taught him the skills needed to hunt and survive in the isolated woods around their rural country home. Paul enjoyed being outdoors so much that schoolwork never came easy. He was unable to sit still for a single moment at a time. He never could quite live up to his parents' expectations, especially since they were the pillars of their small community. After graduating, Paul took the fastest route out of town and enlisted in the military.

THE GHOSTS

## MILITARY

Basic training and Infantryman's School at Fort Campbell, Kentucky, went quickly. As a soldier, Paul was quiet and disciplined. After his upbringing, the service was no challenge at all. He received numerous commendations for his commitment to his unit and the service. Still, Paul decided not to re-up.

His mind changed the day he met an instructor from 7th Special Forces Group. The instructor was an expert in hand-to-hand fighting. He was deadly. Paul was so impressed by the skills, discipline, and overall bearing of Captain Mitchell (now a major) that he volunteered for the most grueling 16 weeks of his life at "Brag." He was joining the Green Berets.

During his initial deployment in the African Theater Paul was able to demonstrate the skills that had been burned into him as a child. After two years with 3rd SFG, Paul has been tapped to join the Ghosts.

## DEMEANOR

When not on an operation Paul's country upbringing shows in everything he does. He is quiet and polite, never forgetting his manners. In combat Paul transforms into an intense no-nonsense warrior. He understands the chain of command and follows orders without question. Growing up in the woods has made him into an efficient battlefield hunter. Paul is usually the first to see or contact the bad guys. He always walks the lead.

# Matt Beasley—Rifleman

## STATS

**DOB:** 06/13/82

**Age:** 31

**Rank:** Sergeant

**Service:** U.S. Army, 7th SFG

**Duties:** Rifleman

## PERSONAL

Hailing from a rough inner-city neighborhood in Detroit, Matt was a "latchkey kid" whose parents worked long hard hours and were rarely home. As a result he spent most of his time on the streets. He knew everyone, good and bad, and while he never got involved in their mischief, he always knew what was happening. Over time he became known as a lone wolf: a tough kid who knew how to work the angles and could get anyone to do anything.

School was a breeze. It required little effort and even less time. After high school Matt knew his parents could not afford to send him to college, so he played the only card he knew: he enlisted.

## MILITARY

Matt started his military career as a rifleman with 4th Infantry Division. Matt excelled in all forms of training. Still the lone wolf, he was well-liked by his squad mates yet depended on no one for anything.

In 2002 Matt and his division were deployed for the invasion of Iraq. Jumping off from Kuwait, his mechanized battalion roared north, destroying everything in its path. The fighting was hard but over before he knew it. While in Iraq, Matt was in constant contact with Rangers form the 82nd Airborne Division. He liked their style. They were aggressive and driven, but what he liked most was their ability to work both singularly and as a team.

Matt immediately realized he was meant for the Rangers, so at the end of his tour he transferred to the 82nd. After the instructors witnessed his performance in jump school he was immediately recommended for Ranger training, where again, Matt excelled.

His first deployment with the 82nd was to the Pashtun region of Afghanistan. The ongoing chase for insurgents was a perfect training ground for America's elite soldiers. Matt learned quickly that cover was good; air support was your friend and mistakes usually get you killed. While in Pashtun he also worked closely with Delta Team operators. He like their style; they were no-nonsense professionals, the elite. Matt applied and was accepted to Delta Force. The training at Bragg was brutal, but in the end he made it through. Matt operated in 7th SFG out of Bragg, where he was deployed to Colombia and also provided support to pro-government forces in the Chilean incident in 2009.

## DEMEANOR

Matt is a loner who sees and hears everything around him. His wariness leads him to rarely volunteer for an assignment. He has not commanded anyone, nor does he ever want to. Yet in a fight, he is quietly committed to the team and will never leave anyone behind.

Matt speaks Spanish, Farsi (Persian), and a few Afghan dialects.

# Marcus Brown—Gunner

## STATS

**DOB:** 06/11/83

**Age:** 30

**Rank:** Sergeant

**Service:** U.S. Army, 7th SFG

**Duties:** SAW Gunner, Heavy Support

## PERSONAL

A college football player from Chicago, Marcus Brown comes from an affluent family who wanted him to go into politics, not the Army. Rebelling from an upper-class upbringing, the headstrong Brown dropped out of college and off of the football team to join the Army and lives his job. He prefers the direct approach to situations.

## MILITARY

Marcus wanted action as soon as possible. He did a tour in Iraq with the 2nd Infantry Brigade, where he was nominated for a Silver Star for his action in Fallujah and earned an impressive track record. His bravery and his calm still impress his comrades. But Marcus still wanted more.

He, too, went through selection at Fort Bragg and came out in the top tier. His first assignments with the 7th SFG were in Africa. Carrying a SAW and a huge ammunition stock under the burning desert sun were never a problem for him.

## DEMEANOR

The Army has turned Marcus into a totally reliable guy. He is no longer the jackass he was before; he is now the guy everybody wants in their team.

# Bo Jenkins—Grenadier

## STATS

**DOB:** 05/18/86

**Age:** 27

**Rank:** Sergeant

**Service:** U.S. Army, 7th SFG

**Duties:** Grenadier

## PERSONAL

Bo's parents divorced when he was 10, and he opted to live with his father in Anchorage, Alaska. Soon after they arrived the man found work as a fisherman and would often be at sea for weeks at a time. As a result Bo spent much of his youth living with his aunt. In a place that is dark for months at a time, Bo made the best of his time. He spent long hours in the weight room and developed an intimidating physique.

In high school Bo was more interested in sports and girls than scholastics. Though he avoided trouble due to his easy-going nature, his lack of discipline made it difficult for him to finish any project he started. His father was concerned that he would end up never reaching his potential. Bo loved and respected the man, so when he suggested Bo try the military to give him the focus he lacked, he enlisted.

## MILITARY

Boot camp and basic training were not difficult for Bo, who was used to long hours of physical training and hardship. He excelled in every aspect of training, quickly gaining the respect of peers and the training cadre. In fact, almost from the start, Bo found himself singled out for special duty. Everyone around him knew he could be the next super soldier. By the end of basic, Bo was recommended for Airborne and Ranger training.

As a Ranger with the 101st, Bo's first deployment was in the Philippines as an Airmobile rifleman. He was at home in the jungle. Bo humped through areas with an amount of gear on his load-bearing harness that would cripple a mule. He never seemed to tire and always pushed those around him by his example. The M-4 rifle, with a 40mm underneath, always looked like a toy in his hands.

After the Philippines, Bo was deployed to Indonesia, Eritrea, and Cuba. It was during these missions that the rock-hard, always-steady Bo Jenkins caught the attention of the Ghost team.

## DEMEANOR

Bo is huge. When not on duty he parties with anyone who can stay up with him. On duty he is strong and capable. He fears very little and shows it. Bo is excellent with his weapon and uses it as often as he can. He is a little impatient and can go forward without orders.

# Alicia Diaz—Marksman

## STATS

**DOB:** 09/14/81

**Age:** 32

**Rank:** Sergeant

**Service:** U.S. Army, 7th SFG

**Duties:** Marksman

## MILITARY

Alicia wanted to prove that a woman could easily perform as well if not better than any man in any situation. She joined the Army to prove that and earned a lot of respect in the process.

She wanted to join the elite, first through her marksmanship training. She won the Service Rifle National Long Range Rifle Championship at Camp Perry, Ohio, two years in a row, which is an unprecedented feat.

She joined the 7th SFG in 2005, and her first assignment for the group was in Afghanistan.

## DEMEANOR

Alicia is friendly, but not outgoing, which must be the price to pay when you are one of the few women in the 7th SFG.

## PERSONAL

Alicia Diaz grew up as a tomboy, daughter of a rancher in Texas, where her family still runs a large ranch. Diaz joined the Army to see the world. She is interested in travel and languages, of which she speaks several. Her love of languages is a strong asset to the team. She spends most of her free time traveling in Europe and South America.

# Johnny Hume—Anti-Tank

## STATS

**DOB:** 10/09/82

**Age:** 29

**Rank:** Sergeant

**Service:** U.S. Army, 7th SFG

**Duties:** Demolitions, Heavy Support

## PERSONAL

Born on a sheep ranch south of Salt Lake City, Utah, Johnny Hume was always considered a little wild. As a boy he loved to hunt and explore the local mountains. Each year his favorite holiday was July 4th because he loved to set off fireworks. As John grew older his father, no stranger to explosives, helped his son stage elaborate firework displays each year that attracted people from hundreds of miles.

Johnny excelled in high school and planned to attend MIT upon graduation, but his father had an untimely stroke that left him paralyzed, forcing Johnny to take over the family business. This arrangement lasted three years, with Johnny's life becoming the farm and not much else. A chance visit from a high school friend who'd joined the military planted a seed in Johnny's mind, and soon after his father passed away he sold the family farm, moved his mother to his brother's home in San Francisco, and enlisted.

## MILITARY

Basic training was rough. Older than most of the recruits, and having already run a family business by the time he was 17, John had a difficult time with authority. When they wanted him to go right, he instinctively wanted to jump left. Halfway through he thought he may have made a mistake.

After basic at Fort Leonard, Hume was transferred to the 5th Infantry Brigade in Iraq. Hume performed well and gained the respect of his fellow soldiers. Soon Hume began to specialize in light anti-tank weapons (LAWs). He utilized his LAWs as bunker busters and "Door Knockers." After his tour, while rotated back to the States, Hume saw a bulletin in the barracks for Special Forces recruitment.

As a Green Beret he specialized in heavy weapons and demolitions. Hume completed his language training and was transferred to a troop operating in the Southern Islands of the Philippines and has fought there since.

## DEMEANOR

Johnny tends to talk a lot and can be quite animated. The only time he seems to calm is when working with explosives or lining the rangefinder on his Javelin. He is fluent in Spanish and Tagalog.

# Alex Nolan—Combat Medic

### STATS

**DOB:** 08/28/80

**Age:** 30

**Rank:** Sergeant

**Service:** U.S. Army, 7th SFG

**Duties:** Medic

## MILITARY

After this board-certified family physician completed his residency in family medicine at Madigan Army Medical Center in Fort Lewis, Washington, he volunteered for a humanitarian assistance mission to Eritrea, where he first came into contact with the Ghosts. Impressed by their steely will, he resolved to one day work at their side. Only after he underwent rigorous training with the 36th Area Support Medical Company (Airborne) and did a tour of duty in Asia did he finally land the toughest assignment any field medic can undertake: going into battle with the Ghosts.

## DEMEANOR

Alex never grew past his geeky look, which makes him an easy target for jokes. He tries to compensate by being funnier, and he's always the first to crack a joke.

## PERSONAL

Alex grew up in Boast, Massachusetts, where both his parents were physicians. Alex was very good at school and socialized in the nerdy crowd. The family tradition, medicine, attracted him, but he wanted a sharper edge, something that gave him a true sense of emergency.

# The Arsenal

As with any occupation, the Ghosts rely on a set of tools to help them complete their tasks. Their tools are weapons—and just like in any toolbox, each one has its purpose. As the premier unit in the Special Operations Forces (SOF), the Ghosts have access to a variety of weapons, including those custom-designed for the SOF. The weapons in this chapter have been organized according to type. Each type has its own strengths and weaknesses. Before you select a weapon for a mission, it is important to have an idea of what you will face so you can choose the appropriate weapon for the job. At times, when you face various threats, you may have to compromise with a weapon that may not be the best in any category but is still effective in several situations. Finally, carry weapons that fit your style of play.

# Assault Rifles and Submachine Guns

Most of the primary weapons fit into this category. It includes not only standard military rifles, such as the AK-47 or the A4, but also specially designed weapons customized for Special Operations, such as the SCAR-L and its family of rifles.

Most of the rifles have two or three rates of fire. Semi-automatic mode fires a single bullet with each pull of the trigger. Burst fires three rounds per trigger pull. Full automatic continues to fire as long as the trigger is held down or until the weapon runs out of ammo. Each shot causes recoil on a weapon and throws off the aim a bit. Therefore, successive shots such as with full automatic are much less accurate than the first round. As a result, semi-automatic fire is more accurate than the other types.

## 36K Carbine

**Ammo Type:** 5.56 x 45mm

**Magazine Capacity:** 30

**Optics:** 3.0x

**Rate of Fire:** Semi, Full/750 RPM

**Suppressed:** No

The standard rifle of the German special forces, the 36K is a lightweight assault carbine. It features a built-in red-dot sight.

### NOTE

The 36K Carbine is used by the rebels in the single-player campaign. The weapon can often be found near dead rebels. Pick one up if you're low on ammo or simply need a well-balanced rifle.

## A4 Rifle

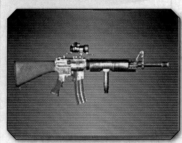

**Ammo Type:** 5.56 x 45mm

**Magazine Capacity:** 30

**Optics:** 3.0x

**Rate of Fire:** Semi, Burst

**Suppressed:** No

A modern variant of the A2 Rifle that has been used by the U.S. Army for decades, the A4 has good accuracy and low recoil but is restricted to burst and semi-automatic fire.

### NOTE

The lack of a fully automatic rate of fire can be frustrating in multiplayer games set in confined areas. Weapons with an automatic fire mode work better in close-quarters encounters.

## AK-47

**Ammo Type:** 7.62 x 39mm

**Magazine Capacity:** 30

**Optics:** None

**Rate of Fire:** Semi, Full/700 RPM

**Suppressed:** No

The standard weapon of the former Soviet bloc since the 1960s, the classic AK-47 provides a reliable infantry weapon, although it is not known for its accuracy.

## NOTE

The AK-47, with its large-caliber round, is one of the most powerful assault rifles available. When fired automatically, it is not very accurate. Fire in short bursts from a crouched or prone position for better control.

# AK-74SU

**Ammo Type:** 5.45 x 39mm

**Magazine Capacity:** 30

**Optics:** None

**Rate of Fire:** Semi, Full/ 700 RPM

**Suppressed:** No

The AK-74SU has a special bell-mouthed flash suppressor necessitated by its extremely short barrel. The lightweight, short assault rifle is still effective to 500 meters.

# AG A3

**Ammo Type:** 5.56 x 45mm

**Magazine Capacity:** 30

**Optics:** 2.0x, 4.0x

**Rate of Fire:** Semi, Full/ 650 RPM

**Suppressed:** No

The AG A3 is a versatile weapon that is easily handled. It has many polymer components in the stock and a clear plastic magazine. It is used by armies and police forces worldwide.

# Cx4 Storm

**Ammo Type:** 4.6 x 30mm

**Magazine Capacity:** 25

**Optics:** 3.0x

**Rate of Fire:** Semi, Burst, Full/700 RPM

**Suppressed:** No

Lightweight, compact, and accurate, the Cx4 Storm was designed with controls similar to those of the M9 pistol. It features a unique camouflage pattern on the stock.

# Cx4 Storm SD

**Ammo Type:** 4.6 x 30mm SS

**Magazine Capacity:** 25

**Optics:** 3.0x

**Rate of Fire:** Semi, Full/ 700 RPM

**Suppressed:** Yes

The suppressed version of the Cx4 Storm brings an added dimension of stealth to this already-lethal platform.

# FAMAS

**Ammo Type:** 5.56 x 45mm

**Magazine Capacity:** 30

**Optics:** 3.0x

**Rate of Fire:** Semi, Burst, Full/900 RPM

**Suppressed:** No

The FAMAS can be shot from either shoulder without any modifications. The versatile bullpup has a high rate of fire and is primarily used by the French military.

# M468

**Ammo Type:** 6.8 x 43mm

**Magazine Capacity:** 28

**Optics:** 3.0x

**Rate of Fire:** Semi, Full/ 750 RPM

**Suppressed:** No

The updated version of the standard U.S. carbine uses a larger round to provide greater lethality against both armored and unarmored targets.

# M468 SD

**Ammo Type:** 6.8 x 43mm SS

**Magazine Capacity:** 28

**Optics:** 3.0x

**Rate of Fire:** Semi, Full/750 RPM

**Suppressed:** Yes

An updated version of the standard U.S. carbine, the M468 SD fires an updated subsonic version of the 6.8mm round for a good combination of lethality and quiet operation.

# M-556

**Ammo Type:** 5.56 x 45mm

**Magazine Capacity:** 30

**Optics:** 3.0x

**Rate of Fire:** Semi, Full/ 750 RPM

**Suppressed:** No

Like many modern assault weapons, the M-556 has many polymer components for weight savings. It has a high rate of fire and a high degree of customization.

# MK14 EBR

**Ammo Type:** 7.62 x 51mm

**Magazine Capacity:** 20

**Optics:** 2.0x, 4.0x

**Rate of Fire:** Semi, Burst, Full/750 RPM

**Suppressed:** No

Designed to replace the M14, the MK14 EBR is now fielded by elements of the U.S. military. The MK14 EBR is lighter, shorter in length, and features more customization than the M14.

# MP5A3 SD

**Ammo Type:** 9 x 19mm SS

**Magazine Capacity:** 30

**Optics:** None

**Rate of Fire:** Semi, Burst, Full/750 RPM

**Suppressed:** Yes

Compact and whisper quiet, this submachine gun is reliable and deadly in close-range engagements but lacks the power and accuracy of most rifles.

## NOTE

The MP5 SD's integrated suppressor reduces sound and completely eliminates muzzle flash. This makes it a popular choice in multiplayer matches where stealth is critical. You can also select the non-silenced version in the single-player campaign.

# MR-C

**Ammo Type:** 5.56 x 25mm

**Magazine Capacity:** 50

**Optics:** 2.0x, 4.0x

**Rate of Fire:** Semi, Full/ 900 RPM

**Suppressed:** No

The Modular Rifle-Caseless is a lightweight weapon with a large, 50-round magazine. Although it maintains decent accuracy, its high rate of fire can make it harder to control than other infantry rifles.

# MR-C LW SD

**Ammo Type:** 5.56 x 25mm

**Magazine Capacity:** 50

**Optics:** None

**Rate of Fire:** Full/900 RPM

**Suppressed:** No

This variant of the MR-C has a camera attached to it. Although it adds bulk, the camera enhances the survivability of the soldier carrying it by allowing him or her to look around corners without being exposed.

## NOTE

This rifle is available in the single-player campaign. Featuring a gun camera, the MR-C LW can be held around corners or over low walls. This allows you to stay behind cover while monitoring or engaging enemies.

# P90/P90SD

**Ammo Type:** 5.7 x 28mm

**Magazine Capacity:** 50

**Optics:** 2.0x, 4.0x

**Rate of Fire:** Semi, Full/ 900 RPM

**Suppressed:** No/Yes

The P90 is a selective-fire, delayed blowback-operated firearm with both semi- and fully automatic firing modes. It is fully ambidextrous and comes in standard and suppressed versions.

# Rx4 Storm

**Ammo Type:** 6.8 x 43mm

**Magazine Capacity:** 28

**Optics:** 2.0x, 4.0x

**Rate of Fire:** Semi, Full/700 RPM

**Suppressed:** No

The Rx4 Storm is designed with the most advanced technology in mind and uses the ARGO system to improve cycling and reliability. Minimized vibration makes it easier to handle and operate.

## NOTE

The Rx4 Storm is a good rifle. Its large-caliber round lets you take down an enemy quicker, and its design is much more stable than some other assault rifles.

# Rx4 Storm SD

**Ammo Type:** 6.8 x 43mm SS

**Magazine Capacity:** 28

**Optics:** 2.0x, 4.0x

**Rate of Fire:** Semi, Full/ 700 RPM

**Suppressed:** Yes

Quiet and lethal describes the suppressed Rx4 Storm. The positioning of its gas valves allows it to be compact and lightweight.

# SA-80

**Ammo Type:** 5.56 x 45mm

**Magazine Capacity:** 30

**Optics:** 2.0x, 4.0x

**Rate of Fire:** Semi, Full/680 RPM

**Suppressed:** No

The standard rifle of the British Army, the SA-80 has recently undergone several reliability upgrades. It is a bullpup design that features a standard optical sight.

# SCAR-H/ SCAR-H SV

**Ammo Type:** 7.62 x 51mm

**Magazine Capacity:** 20

**Optics:** 2.0x, 4.0x

**Rate of Fire:** Semi, Full/600 RPM

**Suppressed:** No

The SCAR-H is the heavy-hitting version of the SCAR-L, chambered for the 7.62 NATO round. It has more stopping power and range, but less ammo and higher recoil. The SV version comes with a standard barrel and improved optics, making it better for long-range shooting.

## NOTE

The SCAR-H fires one of the largest rounds for an assault rifle and is extremely powerful. The downside is a limited 20-round magazine and harsh recoil. Operate the weapon in semi-automatic mode to conserve ammo and keep it on target.

# SCAR-L Carbine

**Ammo Type:** 5.56 x 45mm

**Magazine Capacity:** 30

**Optics:** 3.0x

**Rate of Fire:** Semi, Full/ 750 RPM

**Suppressed:** No

The Special Operations Forces Combat Assault Rifle was developed for U.S. SOF. Its design features power, impact, and versatility.

# SCAR-LCQC

**Ammo Type:** 5.56 x 45mm SS

**Magazine Capacity:** 30

**Optics:** 3.0x

**Rate of Fire:** Semi, Full/ 750 RPM

**Suppressed:** Yes

This compact version of the SCAR-L has an even shorter barrel, with a suppressor attached for quiet fire. It is slightly less accurate and powerful than the standard model.

# SR-3

**Ammo Type:** 9 x 39mm

**Magazine Capacity:** 20

**Optics:** None

**Rate of Fire:** Semi, Full/900 RPM

**Suppressed:** No

Issued to Russian special forces, this small weapon has a high rate of fire and is rumored to defeat body armor at ranges less than 400 meters.

# T-95

**Ammo Type:** 5.8 x 42mm

**Magazine Capacity:** 30

**Optics:** None

**Rate of Fire:** Semi, Full/700 RPM

**Suppressed:** No

Developed by China in the late 1990s, the Type 95 is a bullpup rifle that fires a high-velocity 5.8mm round.

# Grenade Launchers and Anti-Tank Weapons

There are times when you need some heavier firepower on the battlefield than an assault rifle can provide. Grenade launchers offer a hefty offensive punch, particularly when it comes to engaging vehicles and large groups of infantry. Most of these launchers fire high-explosive grenades through a tube mounted beneath the barrel of the weapon. One is a dedicated grenade launcher that can fire either high-explosive or smoke grenades. The arc-like trajectory of a launched grenade requires you to elevate the weapon's barrel when firing on distant targets. At closer ranges, grenades can be fired directly at targets. Correctly ranging a grenade launcher takes some practice and a degree of intuition, but once it is mastered, you can nail targets at long range with devastating (and demoralizing) results. Also included in this category are a couple of anti-tank rocket launchers.

# A4 RIFLE/M320

**Ammo Type:** 5.56 x 45mm/40mm

**Magazine Capacity:** 30

**Optics:** 3.0x

**Rate of Fire:** Semi, Burst

**Suppressed:** No

An advancement of the classic A2 Rifle/M203 combo in use since Vietnam, this platform provides lightweight and accurate direct and indirect fire.

# Cx4 STORM/XL6

**Ammo Type:** 4.6 x 30mm/40mm

**Magazine Capacity:** 25

**Optics:** 3.0x

**Rate of Fire:** Semi, Burst, Full/700 RPM

**Suppressed:** No

Lightweight and compact, the Cx4 Storm/XL6 combines maneuverability with the powerful indirect fire of its under-barrel grenade launcher. It features a unique camouflage pattern on the stock.

# AG A3/SGL

**Ammo Type:** 5.56 x 45mm/40mm

**Magazine Capacity:** 30

**Optics:** 2.0x, 4.0x

**Rate of Fire:** Semi, Full/650 RPM

**Suppressed:** No

The AG A3/SGL combines the highly accurate AG A3 with the brute strength of a 40mm grenade launcher.

# FAMAS/M204

**Ammo Type:** 5.56 x 45mm/40mm

**Magazine Capacity:** 30

**Optics:** 3.0x

**Rate of Fire:** Semi, Burst, Full/980 RPM

**Suppressed:** No

The addition of a grenade launcher makes the FAMAS/M204 an extremely powerful weapons platform, with a cyclic fire rate approaching 1,000 rounds per minute (RPM).

## M-32 MGL

**Ammo Type:** 40mm

**Magazine Capacity:** 6

**Optics:** 3.0x

**Rate of Fire:** Semi

**Suppressed:** No

The M-32 MGL Six Pack is a deadly fire support weapon that can devastate a target area in seconds with six 40mm grenades. It has recently been adopted for use by the U.S. military.

## M-32 MGL Smoke

**Ammo Type:** 40mm

**Magazine Capacity:** 6

**Optics:** 3.0x

**Rate of Fire:** Semi

**Suppressed:** No

This variant of the M-32 carries only 40mm smoke grenades for concealment.

## M468/M320

**Ammo Type:** 6.8 x 43mm/40mm

**Magazine Capacity:** 28

**Optics:** 3.0x

**Rate of Fire:** Semi, Full/ 750 RPM

**Suppressed:** No

The standard M468 with attached M320 grenade launcher provides a versatile dual-purpose platform.

## M468 SD/M320

**Ammo Type:** 6.8 x 43mm SS/40mm

**Magazine Capacity:** 28

**Optics:** 3.0x

**Rate of Fire:** Semi, Full/ 750 RPM

**Suppressed:** Yes

Combining a heavy grenade launcher with a suppressed weapon provides a maximum amount of tactical flexibility for diverse situations.

## M-556/M320

**Ammo Type:** 5.56 x 45mm/40mm

**Magazine Capacity:** 30

**Optics:** 3.0x

**Rate of Fire:** Semi, Full/ 750 RPM

**Suppressed:** No

This deadly variant of the M-556 couples the accuracy of the basic rifle with the added indirect fire support of a 40mm grenade launcher.

## MR-C/AGL

**Ammo Type:** 5.56 x 45mm/40mm

**Optics:** 2.0x, 4.0x

**Rate of Fire:** Semi, Full/900 RPM

**Suppressed:** No

Coupling the high rate of fire of the MR-C with a 40mm grenade launcher provides a tremendous amount of firepower.

## Rx4 Storm/XL7

**Ammo Type:** 6.8 x 43mm/40mm

**Magazine Capacity:** 28

**Optics:** 2.0x, 4.0x

**Rate of Fire:** Semi, Full/ 700 RPM

**Suppressed:** No

This rifle was designed with the most advanced technology in mind and using the ARGO system to improve cycling and reliability; the further addition of a 40mm grenade launcher makes for a devastating combination.

## SA-80/M320

**Ammo Type:** 5.56 x 45mm/40mm

**Magazine Capacity:** 30

**Optics:** 2.0x, 4.0x

**Rate of Fire:** Semi, Full/680 RPM

**Suppressed:** No

Even with the addition of an under-barrel grenade launcher, the SA-80's bullpup design provides a compact combat package.

# SCAR-L/EGLM

**Ammo Type:** 5.56 x 45mm/40mm

**Magazine Capacity:** 30

**Optics:** None

**Rate of Fire:** Semi, Full/ 750 RPM

**Suppressed:** No

This SCAR-L is fitted with an under-barrel 40mm grenade launcher for heavy indirect fire.

# SCAR-LCQC/EGLM

**Ammo Type:** 5.56 x 45mm/40mm SS

**Magazine Capacity:** 30

**Optics:** None

**Rate of Fire:** Semi, Full/ 750 RPM

**Suppressed:** Yes

This variant of the SCAR-L comes equipped with an under-barrel grenade launcher. Combining a suppressed rifle with the firepower of a grenade launcher makes it a versatile and lethal weapon system.

# T-95/M320

**Ammo Type:** 5.8 x 42mm/40mm

**Magazine Capacity:** 30

**Optics:** None

**Rate of Fire:** Semi, Full/ 700 RPM

**Suppressed:** No

With an adapter, the T-95 mounts the lightweight M320 grenade launcher, for heavy indirect fire support.

# ZEUS MPAR

**Ammo Type:** 84mm HE

**Magazine Capacity:** 1

**Optics:** 4.0x

**Rate of Fire:** Semi

**Suppressed:** No

The Zeus MPAR is a new anti-armor system designed to provide the portability of the AT4 anti-tank weapon within a multi-use reloadable package, capable of destroying armored vehicles.

# ZEUS T2

**Ammo Type:** 137mm

**Magazine Capacity:** 1

**Optics:** 4.0x

**Rate of Fire:** Semi

**Suppressed:** No

Useful against heavily armored vehicles, this guided weapon delivers massive, directed firepower. Maintaining the aim on the target guides the ordnance in.

## NOTE

The T2 version is available in the single-player campaign, while the MPAR is for the multiplayer game. Both are radio-controlled rockets that can be guided toward a target by the user keeping the target centered in the sights until impact. The Zeus will destroy most vehicles, including helicopters, with a single hit. Tanks, however, require two hits.

# Light Machine Guns

Light machine guns are designed to put out a heavy amount of firepower. As such, they are designed to be fired on full automatic and have large magazines allowing a soldier to continue to fire a lot of rounds before having to reload. The trade-offs for these abilities are heavy recoil and decreased accuracy. However, this type of weapon is intended to suppress enemies, forcing them to keep their heads down and preventing them from attacking while friendly soldiers maneuver to carry out their own attack. Some of these light machine guns are merely modified assault rifles, while others are dedicated LMGs. To improve accuracy, fire these weapons from a prone position.

## AK-47 LMG

**Ammo Type:** 7.62 x 39mm

**Magazine Capacity:** 75

**Optics:** None

**Rate of Fire:** Semi, Full/ 700 RPM

**Suppressed:** No

Modified from the classic AK-47, the AK-47 LMG includes a 75-round drum magazine and shares most of the characteristics of the AK-47.

## A556 SAW

**Ammo Type:** 5.56 x 45mm

**Magazine Capacity:** 100

**Optics:** None

**Rate of Fire:** Full/850 RPM

**Suppressed:** No

The A556 SAW combines a large effective range in a lightweight customizable package. The heavy firepower it provides is ideal for enemy suppression.

## M36 SAW

**Ammo Type:** 5.56 x 45mm

**Magazine Capacity:** 100

**Optics:** None

**Rate of Fire:** Semi, Burst, Full/750 RPM

**Suppressed:** No

This variant of the 36K features a 100-round C magazine. The added weight is offset by the devastating volume of fire the extra ammunition provides.

## MG21

**Ammo Type:** 7.62 x 51mm

**Magazine Capacity:** 100

**Optics:** None

**Rate of Fire:** Full/850 RPM

**Suppressed:** No

Although a very heavy LMG, the MG21 makes up for it by being very controllable in automatic fire.

## M60

**Ammo Type:** 7.62 x 51mm

**Magazine Capacity:** 100

**Optics:** None

**Rate of Fire:** Full/750 RPM

**Suppressed:** No

An updated version of the classic LMG, the M60 is designed for heavy suppression fire, fed from a 100-round belt.

## MK48 LMG

**Ammo Type:** 7.62 x 51mm

**Magazine Capacity:** 100

**Optics:** None

**Rate of Fire:** Full/850 RPM

**Suppressed:** No

The MK48 is a new light machine gun, designed to provide heavy firepower in a light and portable platform.

THE ARSENAL

# T-95 LMG

**Ammo Type:** 5.8 x 42mm

**Magazine Capacity:** 75

**Optics:** None

**Rate of Fire:** Full/750 RPM

**Suppressed:** No

## NOTE

Though its magazine holds only 75 rounds (compared to the 100-round magazines used by other weapons in this class) and it fires a smaller-caliber round, the T-95 LMG is much more accurate.

A variant of the T-95 rifle, the T-95 light machine gun features a 75-round drum magazine and is a compact and maneuverable support weapon.

# Sniper Rifles

Sniper rifles are extremely accurate and feature sights with increased magnification to allow for attacking hostiles at long range. Since accuracy is most important, all of these rifles can only fire one shot at a time. Sniper rifles come in various designs. Some are compact and light for use in urban settings, where speed is more important than range or stopping power. Others fire a large round capable of penetrating walls and causing damage to vehicles. These are especially useful in the counter-sniper role.

## DSR-1

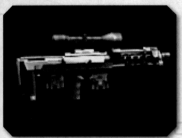

**Ammo Type:** .338 Lapua

**Magazine Capacity:** 4

**Optics:** 4.0x, 16.0x

**Rate of Fire:** Semi

**Suppressed:** No

The DSR-1 rifle has been called "the most sophisticated and technologically advanced tactical precision rifle in the world." It has been designed to meet or exceed all mission requirements for a tactical precision rifle.

## KJY-88 Sniper

**Ammo Type:** 5.8 x 42mm

**Magazine Capacity:** 10

**Optics:** 8.0x, 16.0x

**Rate of Fire:** Semi

**Suppressed:** No

The sniper variant of the T-95 rifle was designed to replace the SVD Sniper. It fires the high-velocity 5.8mm round and is both lighter and more accurate than the SVD.

## M-556 SL

**Ammo Type:** 5.56 x 45mm

**Magazine Capacity:** 30

**Optics:** 8.0x, 16.0x

**Rate of Fire:** Semi

**Suppressed:** No

This medium-range sniper rifle is a long-barreled version of the M-556. It has a semi-automatic action that allows for speedy follow-up shots. It was designed to be used by specially trained Swiss police forces.

## M95 Sniper

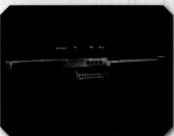

**Ammo Type:** 12.7 x 99mm

**Magazine Capacity:** 6

**Optics:** 4.0x, 16.0x

**Rate of Fire:** Semi

**Suppressed:** No

The M95 is a compact, bullpup, bolt-action sniper rifle designed to fit into a small case. Fire from this weapon can pierce thin walls and take out enemies behind them.

# M107 Sniper

**Ammo Type:** 12.7 x 99mm

**Magazine Capacity:** 10

**Optics:** 8.0x, 16.0x

**Rate of Fire:** Semi

**Suppressed:** No

Recently officially adopted by the U.S. military, the M107 has long been in use as the heavy sniper rifle of choice; it features semi-automatic fire from a 10-round magazine.

# SR 25 Sniper

**Ammo Type:** 7.62 x 51mm

**Magazine Capacity:** 20

**Optics:** 8.0x, 16.0x

**Rate of Fire:** Semi

**Suppressed:** No

Built on the standard A2 Rifle platform, the SR 25 fires a more potent round and features a heavy barrel for accurate fire.

# SR 25 SD Sniper

**Ammo Type:** 7.62 x 51mm SS

**Magazine Capacity:** 20

**Optics:** 8.0x, 16.0x

**Rate of Fire:** Semi

**Suppressed:** Yes

Combining the power of the SR 25 rifle with a suppressor, the SR 25 SD Sniper rifle is lethal, accurate, and quiet.

# SR A550

**Ammo Type:** 12.7 x 99mm

**Magazine Capacity:** 5

**Optics:** 8.0x, 16.0x

**Rate of Fire:** Semi

**Suppressed:** No

Built for Special Operations counter-sniper and anti-vehicular fire, the SR A550 is both powerful and accurate at long ranges. This weapon can pierce thin walls and shoot hidden enemies.

## NOTE

The powerful A550 is the rifle used for counter-sniping in the single-player campaign. When you're counter-sniping, a target's silhouette is visible through the scope, even when the target is hidden behind cover. Engaging a target through cover significantly reduces the velocity of the bullet, as it must first pass through the cover material before entering the target. Therefore, the bullet causes less damage than normal. However, you can ensure a kill every time by going for a head shot.

# SVD Sniper

**Ammo Type:** 7.62 x 54mm

**Magazine Capacity:** 10

**Optics:** 8.0x, 16.0x

**Rate of Fire:** Semi

**Suppressed:** No

The SVD Sniper has had an impressive length of service since its original introduction to the Soviet military in 1963. It has been upgraded over time to meet the changing demands of the countries that continue to field it.

# VSK-50 Sniper

**Ammo Type:** 12.7 x 97mm SS

**Magazine Capacity:** 5

**Optics:** 8.0x, 16.0x

**Rate of Fire:** Semi

**Suppressed:** Yes

Developed by special request from the Russian Federal Security Service, the VSK-50 Sniper is a silenced sniper rifle used for counter-terrorist operations.

# Other Weapons

Some weapons are intended in a supporting role. These include pistols as well as grenades and explosives. Pistols are best used at close range and as a fall-back weapon for times when you run out of ammo for your primary weapon or for personal defense when your primary weapon is not intended for close combat.

## ICQB

**Ammo Type:** 0.45 ACP

**Magazine Capacity:** 7

**Optics:** None

**Rate of Fire:** Semi

**Suppressed:** No

The Interim Close Quarter Battle pistol marks the return of the U.S. military to issuing .45-caliber sidearms to its members.

## ICQB SD

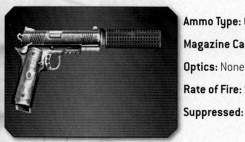

**Ammo Type:** 0.45 SS ACP

**Magazine Capacity:** 7

**Optics:** None

**Rate of Fire:** Semi

**Suppressed:** Yes

Subsonic ammunition makes this silenced version of the ICQB a stealthy weapon to be feared by opponents.

## M9

**Ammo Type:** 9 x 19mm

**Magazine Capacity:** 15

**Optics:** None

**Rate of Fire:** Semi

**Suppressed:** No

The M9 pistol is the standard sidearm of the U.S. military. It has a high magazine capacity and low recoil.

## M9 SD

**Ammo Type:** 9 x 19mm SS

**Magazine Capacity:** 15

**Optics:** None

**Rate of Fire:** Semi

**Suppressed:** Yes

This M9 pistol is fitted with a suppressor for quiet fire, with a corresponding lessening of power and recoil.

## Px4 Storm

**Ammo Type:** 4.6 x 30mm

**Magazine Capacity:** 20

**Optics:** None

**Rate of Fire:** Semi

**Suppressed:** No

With an increased magazine capacity and no-glare camouflage-pattern finish, the Px4 Storm is an excellent military sidearm.

## Px4 Storm SD

**Ammo Type:** 4.6 x 30mm SS

**Magazine Capacity:** 20

**Optics:** None

**Rate of Fire:** Semi

**Suppressed:** Yes

The increased magazine capacity of the Px4 Storm coupled with a suppressor makes this pistol a great choice for close-quarters combat.

## M1014

**Ammo Type:** 4-inch Shell

**Magazine Capacity:** 6

**Optics:** None

**Rate of Fire:** Semi

**Suppressed:** No

The M1014 is a powerful semi-automatic shotgun, supremely lethal in close-combat situations.

# M18 Claymore

Consisting of a shaped charge directing metal BBs in a wide arc in front of it, the claymore mine is an ideal weapon to use against groups of enemies.

## NOTE

The claymore is available only for multiplayer games. It is a good weapon for setting up an ambush and can kill at a range of several meters.

# M67 Grenade

The M67 fragmentation grenade is the standard issue anti-personnel grenade used by U.S. forces.

## NOTE

Frag grenades detonate by a timed fuse rather than on impact. Therefore, you can throw them so they bounce off of a wall or roll under a vehicle. They are most effective indoors, where the confined space keeps the targets and the grenade in close proximity. However, they can also be useful for killing enemies behind cover.

# Smoke Grenade

The basic smoke grenade continues to prove its worth on the modern battlefield by obscuring the enemy's vision and allowing soldiers to maneuver without being seen.

## NOTE

In addition to concealing movement, smoke is also useful whenever you're pinned or facing superior firepower. Place a smoke screen between yourself and the enemy to halt incoming fire. Then use your thermal vision to see through the smoke and engage the hostiles.

# Satchel Charge

A satchel charge is a powerful, portable explosive device. It is used by infantry and airborne troops to demolish heavy stationary targets such as vehicles, obstacles, blockhouses, bunkers, caves, and bridges.

# C4

The U.S. Army's M183 satchel charge contains a high amount of plastic explosive primed with a timed fuse. It can destroy armored vehicles.

## NOTE

In some single-player campaign missions, you use C4 charges equipped with timers. Even though these charges aren't visible in your inventory, the explosives are automatically available during certain objectives.

THE ARSENAL

# The Campaign

Captain Scott Mitchell and the Ghosts have completed their assignment in Mexico City. However, they have no time for some R and R. The civil war in Mexico is threatening the security of the United States, and only a unit like the Ghosts can deal with these enemies.

## Battle Simulator

### OBJECTIVES

1. Rendezvous with Allied Force
2. Ambush Enemy Convoy
3. Reach Ramirez's Position
4. Secure Tequila Factory Area
5. Move to LZ 2 for Extraction

### MISSION BRIEFING

Simulation Zone: Juarez Mexico 31.40N 106.28W

**You will be training in a simulation of Juarez, Mexico.**

To hone his skills and prepare for the upcoming missions, Captain Mitchell has been ordered to go through the battle simulator. In addition to allowing him to practice the tactics he used in Mexico City, the simulator provides training in some new features and equipment the Ghosts can use in combat. The simulator features four different exercises, which are called workshops. Many are extremely realistic and should be treated as actual combat. Josh Rosen leads you through these workshops. Josh will be your data man during missions. Listen to his advice.

## WORKSHOP 1: COMBAT BASICS

#### MAP SECTION A

The training is set to simulate Juarez, Mexico—the border town around which you will be operating. The first workshop is fairly basic and focuses on movement, cover, and using firearms.

Your objective is designated by a yellow square on your HUD. This is the point you have to reach.

**Follow the yellow squares on the HUD to your objectives.**

During missions, objectives are designated on your heads-up display, or HUD, with a yellow square. When you aim the reticle at the square, it reveals information about the objective, including its distance from your current location. Your first objective is to the north. Walk to it to receive another objective.

If the objective is not directly visible, its direction will be indicated by a yellow arrow on one side of the HUD, showing you where you must turn to face the objective. Continue to the second objective.

**The tactical map is an invaluable tool during combat.**

During combat, you will need to use your tactical map. This 3D representation shows not only your location but also the locations of your objective, friendly units, and detected enemies. Follow the onscreen directions to open your tactical map. This map is zoomed in by default but can be zoomed out to see the bigger picture. When other assets have been assigned to your command, you can give them orders using the tactical map. This view also lists your current objectives.

## NOTE

The tactical map also shows the limits of the battle-field. Gray areas are outside the fighting area. If you enter a gray area, the mission will be canceled. Orange zones indicate hostile areas where you can expect to find the enemy, while blue zones are secured terrain—usually an area that you have previously cleared of enemy resistance.

Close the tactical map. It is now time to use your weapon. Follow the onscreen directions to use aim mode. Note that the four dashes of the reticle are now connected to form a yellow circle. This indicates that you are taking aim at a target. As a result, your accuracy is increased. When firing at the enemy, always try to use aim mode. The only downside is that you can't move as quickly. A cardboard box with a target on it is to the east of your current position. Take aim at it and fire.

**Aim mode**

**Move to this wall and take cover behind it.**

Your next objective is a wall to the northeast. Move to the wall and continue to walk right into it to pin yourself against it. This places you behind cover. One of the fundamentals of military operations, especially those in an urban environment, is that the one with the best cover wins. Using cover makes it more difficult for the enemy to hit you. However, not all types of cover are equal. Brick or concrete is best. Thinner materials such as wood can be penetrated by bullets, so avoid using these for cover.

**Use aim mode as you shoot around the corner at the box.**

Once in cover, you can move to the edges to peek around. Move to the left or right edge and press the button to enter aim mode. Now fire at another cardboard box target. While shooting at a target from behind cover, part of your body is exposed and vulnerable to enemy fire. Therefore, when engaging the enemy, take your shot and then move back behind cover.

**Move to his low wall and use it for cover.**

**Glance over the wall and shoot the three targets.**

Follow the directions to leave cover and then reload your weapon. It is a good habit to check your ammo level in the lower-right corner of the screen after each engagement. You never want to get into a fight with only a few rounds in the magazine. Now head to the next objective and take cover behind a stone wall. Besides peeking around cover, you can also glance over lower cover such as this wall. Look over the wall, take aim, and shoot the three targets.

**Climb over the low wall.**

THE CAMPAIGN

You can also climb over low walls. Scramble over the wall and move toward the next objective. Along the way, try changing your stance. While you can move faster upright, a crouch is a safer way to move through enemy territory since you are more difficult for the enemy to see and are also harder to hit. Go ahead and stand up and continue down the alley to the test phase of this first workshop.

**Head down the alley to the next objective.**

As you approach the end of the alley, Rosen informs you that an enemy patrol is along the street ahead of you. This is your first test. To master it, you must eliminate all five enemies without taking a single hit yourself. (Mastery also earns you an achievement in the Xbox 360 version.) Remember to use cover.

**Locate the enemies in the street while behind cover, and then peek around the corner to take them out.**

**Reload while behind cover and before advancing so you are sure to have a full magazine for the next engagement.**

Take cover along the wall on the alley's northern side and move toward the corner. Since you have a third-person view of the scene, you can actually see around the corner without exposing your character. There are two enemies down the street. Notice that once you locate them, a red intel marker appears over them in your HUD. Peek around the corner and take aim at one of the enemies. The intel diamond changes to a targeting bracket that identifies the enemy and lists his health as a percentage. Fire at the target until the health decreases to zero. As you open fire, the enemies usually try to seek cover and return fire.

**This kiosk also provides good cover.**

It is possible to take out both enemies from this corner. However, the second one can be tough depending on where he takes cover. You may have to cross the street and take cover behind the metal newspaper kiosk. Before you cross the street, stand up so you can run across, minimizing the amount of time you are out in the open.

Seek cover behind this van while you go after the third hostile.

Notice how your HUD shows the outline of the hostile in red. This allows you to monitor the movements of an enemy and ready your aim so you can hit him when he pokes his head around the corner.

Now move to take cover behind the rusted shell of a van along the left side of the street. As you approach the van, the third enemy reveals himself. Try to take him down while he is out in the open. However, if he gets behind cover, take aim and wait for him to show himself as he tries to take a shot at you.

Only two more left. Take out one of them while they are out in the open.

Three enemies are now down—only two remain. Advance down the street again and take cover behind a stack of lumber. While wooden walls can be penetrated by bullets, these sturdy posts provide great protection. Two enemies walk back and forth across the street. You can either peek around the right corner of the lumber or glance over the top. Shoot one while they are out in the open. The second usually hides behind an old pickup truck. As before, wait until he exposes part of his body and then fire. It may take a few shots to eliminate him. After all five have been taken down, Josh will give you the results of the test.

The results of the workshop. Your score is based on how many hits you take.

# WORKSHOP 2: SNIPING

**MAP SECTION A**

Head up these stairs to the next training.

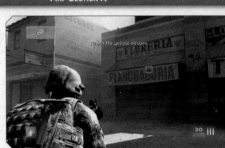

Pick up the rifle and select single-shot rate of fire.

The next workshop trains you in attacking targets at long range. Move toward the objective icon in your HUD. At the top of the stairs, you will find a rifle—an MK14 EBR. Pick it up. Since this rifle has different rates of fire, you can set it for the type of action in which you will be engaging. For long-range firing, select single shot. Now take cover behind the wall. As you glance over the top of the wall, press the scope button to look through your weapon's sight. Some weapons have more than one magnification setting, and pressing the scope button again increases the magnification. However, your rifle has only one level. Pressing the scope button again returns you to the normal view.

**Take cover behind this wall.**

**Watch the air reserve meter at the bottom of the scope while holding your breath.**

While looking through the scope, locate the cardboard boxes on the adjacent building. To increase your accuracy, hold your breath by holding down the aim mode button. Notice the air reserve meter at the bottom of the scope view. As you hold your breath, the meter decreases and changes from green to yellow, and then to red. Once in the red, you are in need of a breath and your accuracy decreases again. Release the aim mode button to breathe freely again. Try holding your breath and observing the effects on your reticle. After you get the hang of it, shoot the targets to continue.

**Use the tactical map to see the where the buildings are located along the way to the top of the hill and plan your movement from cover to cover.**

Now exit scope view and head down the stairs to the next objective location. This is the test portion of the workshop. You must neutralize five sentries on the way to the hillside. However, for scoring purposes, only head shots count. To get a perfect score and master this workshop, you must get five head shots.

**Locate the enemy around the corner, then use the scope to make the head shot.**

### NOTE

If you miss the target's head and only hit the body, you will cause damage to the enemy but won't kill him with a single shot. Therefore, during combat, head shots prevent the enemy from running for cover and from returning fire.

Move toward the building near the objective marker. Take cover along the wall on the left side and look around the corner. The first enemy sentry is on a rooftop to the east. While peeking around the corner, press the scope button and take aim at the enemy. Hold your breath and aim for the head. If you hit the head, you will kill the enemy with a single shot. Advance to the building where the first sentry was located and take up a position along the right side of the porch, using it for cover as you engage the second sentry on the building to the south. Use the same tactic as before to score a second head shot.

**Take the time to center the crosshair right over the target's head.**

The third sentry is on the rooftop of a building to the east. You can try to shoot him from this same location—a longer shot—or move a bit closer. To move closer, go around the building's northern side and advance to the next building to the east. Take up a cover position along the right side and neutralize the third sentry with a head shot.

**These two sentries are tougher. After you kill one, the other will open fire on your position. Stay behind cover and you will be safe.**

The last two enemies are at the base of the windmill to the east. Advance up the hillside using the stairs made out of old tires to another building, which you can use for cover. Take a shot at one and then move back behind cover since the other sentry will start shooting at you. Once the firing dies down, peek around quickly, look through the scope, and make another head shot to clear this area. Josh will give you your score for this workshop. If you did not get five head shots, consider restarting this workshop and trying again.

**Five headshots makes for a perfect score.**

# WORKSHOP 3: SMOKE AND SATCHELS

## MAP SECTION C

**Move over to these tires and drop prone.**

Advance to the objective marker at the top of the hillside. For this workshop, you practice using stealth techniques to advance on an enemy you can't engage directly. Josh first has you practice changing your stance. You can also drop prone. While prone, you are much more difficult for the enemy to locate and hit. You can also use lower objects for cover. Head over to the small stack of tires and drop prone behind them.

**Throw a smoke grenade while staying prone. Then move forward once smoke obscures the vehicle so it can't see you.**

THE CAMPAIGN

An APC (armored personnel carrier) drives up and stops in front of you. You can't destroy it from this distance, so you must get closer. Select your smoke grenades and then back away from the tires while staying prone until your reticle changes to show that you can use the grenade. Hold down the fire button until the grenade reticle charges up and turns red, then release to throw the smoke grenade toward the APC. Wait for the smoke to build up, and then stand up and move to the next objective location.

Throw a satchel charge and then detonate it.

Take cover behind the wooden fence. Use your enhanced night-vision goggles (ENVG) if necessary to locate the APC through the smoke. Switch to a satchel charge and throw it at the APC. Satchel charges must be detonated. Once you have thrown a charge, you detonate it by pressing the fire button. Detonate the charge to blow up the APC. Once it is smoking, advance to the next objective location. Switch back to your smoke grenades as you go.

Throw a couple of smoke grenades to conceal your movement toward the APC.

Use the wooden fences along the right side for cover as you advance.

Get to the side of the APC. If it sees you, it will drive toward you and start firing. Drop a smoke grenade right next to you if necessary.

Now comes the test part of the workshop. You must engage a hostile APC and destroy it. This time the APC will shoot at you if it can see you. Therefore, you must use cover and smoke to conceal your movements so you can get close enough to use a satchel charge. From this location, peek around the corner of the building and throw one smoke grenade toward the enemy APC and another along the right side of the road. This allows you to move to take cover behind a wooden fence. As the smoke begins to clear, throw smoke grenades into the street and along the right side as you advance. Keep going until you are to the side of the APC. Use your goggles to see through the smoke. Once you are to the side of the APC, throw a satchel charge at it and detonate it. To achieve a perfect score and master this workshop, you must use only one satchel charge to destroy the APC.

# WORKSHOP 4: TEAMWORK

## MAP SECTION D

Your team is waiting for you in the Ghost truck.

Select your teammates and your weapons before continuing the workshop.

The last workshop focuses on commanding your team. Head over to the truck to meet up with your team. When you arrive, a setup console opens. During the campaign, this appears at the beginning of a mission, and some features are available whenever you access one of your team's vehicles or a supply source such as the MULE. The News screen shows information about the mission as well as intel on the battlefield, suspected enemies, and equipment you have available.

Continue past this screen to the Teammates screen, where you can select the members of your team for the current mission. The first tier of teammates lists your riflemen. The second tier lists your heavy weapons' soldiers—your gunner and your grenadier. Select a gunner for this workshop. Finally, the third tier is for support. This workshop allows you to select only the combat medic. However, in the campaign, you can also select a marksman, an anti-tank soldier, or a second rifleman.

Accept these choices to get to the Weapons screen, where you can choose your personal loadout. Normally you would pick a primary weapon, a secondary weapon, and your grenades pack. However, for this workshop, your weapons loadout is set. Accept it to continue to the Summary screen, which shows your selected team and weapons loadout. This lets you review your choices before accepting them and exiting to the mission.

This is your team.

When giving a move order, your HUD will show you the positions to which each Ghost will move. If you don't like it, adjust your reticle and give another move order.

Use the command full view to see what your team can see and give them orders.

THE CAMPAIGN

You now have control of a team of three Ghosts. Notice the Cross-Com in the upper-left corner of the screen. This allows you to cycle through support units, check their status, and give them orders during a mission. It is time to practice giving them orders. Locate the objective square on your HUD. Instead of moving there yourself, follow the onscreen directions to give your teammates a Go To order to move to the position. A new feature is the ability for you to see through your supports' mounted cameras. This is referred to as command full view or CFV. Press the CFV button to see what your team can see. From this view, you can look around and give orders. While in CFV, order your team to Go To the next objective. During combat, you can also use CFV to order your team to attack specific targets.

Exit CFV and, while leaving your team in position, move to the next objective location. Now order your team to Regroup. The squad will move to your position and then continue to follow you until you give a Go To order. Move to the next objective location and watch how your team follows you.

Your team moves to your position when you order them to Regroup.

At any time, you can change the rules of engagement, or ROE, of your team with your Cross-Com. Your team begins in Recon mode by default. While in this mode, they will move about quietly and only fire on enemies that fire on them first. Press the ROE button to switch to Assault mode. Your team will now automatically engage any enemies they see and can fire on.

Order your team to move to this location, from where they will observe enemies and wait for you to switch to Assault mode. They will automatically open fire on enemies in their sight.

Now lead your team to the next objective location and switch them back to Recon mode. Order them to Go To the indicated position on the upper level, then advance on your own to the next objective location at ground level. As you move toward your destination, your team locates a couple of enemies. Red intel diamonds appear on your HUD. Since your team is in Recon mode, they will not fire on these enemies, but just observe them. Press the ROE button to switch your team to Assault mode and watch what happens. They will quickly take down the enemies. By moving into position in Recon mode, they were able to set up for an attack without alerting the enemy. Then once in position, they fired first when you set them to Assault mode. Switch your team back to Recon mode and order them to Regroup on you at the next objective location.

Move your team to this short wall so they can detect hostiles.

You can order your team to fire on a specific hostile with an Attack order.

It is now time for your final workshop test. You must neutralize all hostiles on the way to the gas station. There are five. However, this time you are scored on the number of enemies your team takes out. They must eliminate all five to earn a perfect score. Therefore, don't take out any yourself—just lead your team. Move toward the house to the west and order your team to Go To a position where the wall is shorter. From there, your team will detect two hostiles; however, they will not fire on them since they are still in Recon mode. Switch to Assault mode and they will engage the enemy. You can highlight enemy intel markers on your HUD with your reticle and order your team to attack those targets—even if you can't see them directly. Try using the CFV as well. If your team can't kill these hostiles, order them to move along the wall to the western end (where it is also short) and engage from there.

Send your team forward to clear out the rest of the hostiles.

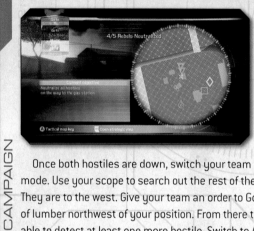

You can also give orders to your team from the tactical map, which provides an overhead view of the battlefield.

Once both hostiles are down, switch your team back to Recon mode. Use your scope to search out the rest of the enemies. They are to the west. Give your team an order to Go To the stack of lumber northwest of your position. From there they should be able to detect at least one more hostile. Switch to Assault mode and order your team to fire on the hostile. Continue advancing them along the southern side of the battlefield, moving from cover to cover. You can also use the tactical map to give them Go To and Attack orders. Work with the tactical map and the CFV until all hostiles have been eliminated. Josh will then give you your score. As long as your team took out all the enemies, you will have a perfect score.

Use the CFV to give an Attack order to your team.

The combat medic is the only soldier capable of healing you.

Though you have completed the test, you still have a few things to learn in this workshop. Order your team to Regroup with you at the next objective location. From there, order them to move into cover near the pickup truck. Activate CFV and locate an enemy truck. Order your team to attack it and then the two hostiles near it. One of your team was wounded during this last engagement. Aim your reticle at the wounded soldier and give the Heal order. Your combat medic will move over and take care of the soldier. If you don't have a combat medic during a mission, another soldier or you can also heal a wounded soldier. To heal someone, approach and then press the action button while the emergency heal intervention contextual icon is present. You were also wounded. You can be healed only by the combat medic—not another one of your soldiers. To order the medic to heal you, aim your reticle at the medic and give the Heal order.

The unmanned aerial vehicle (UAV) can detect enemies for you and continue to monitor them.

Order your team to Regroup and then lead them up the stairs to the rooftop of the building to the north. From here you will learn how to use the Cross-Com to control your UAV recon drone. You can use this drone to fly over the battlefield and locate enemies. Follow the directions to select the UAV from your Cross-Com. Now open the tactical map and order the UAV to Go To the objective location. You can also see what the drone sees by using the CFV. Activate it and the UAV will detect an enemy truck. Then take control of the UAV to fly it toward the next objective location to find another truck. While you are in CFV, the UAV will fly at a lower altitude and allow you to get a better look at the area. However, it is also vulnerable to enemy fire at this low altitude. Once you detect some enemy soldiers, exit CFV so the drone will return to a higher altitude. Though the drone can only detect enemy units at low altitude and show their location with intel markers, it can continue to monitor their location at high altitude as long as the drone or the enemies do not move out of range. Therefore, once you detect hostiles, leave the UAV hovering at high altitude to monitor them. Order the drone to Regroup on your position and then exit the tactical map to end the battle simulation.

THE CAMPAIGN: **BATTLE SIMULATOR**

# Need Your Cojones, Son

## GRAW2 ▶ SINGLE PLAYER
### MISSION 1: NEED YOUR COJONES, SON

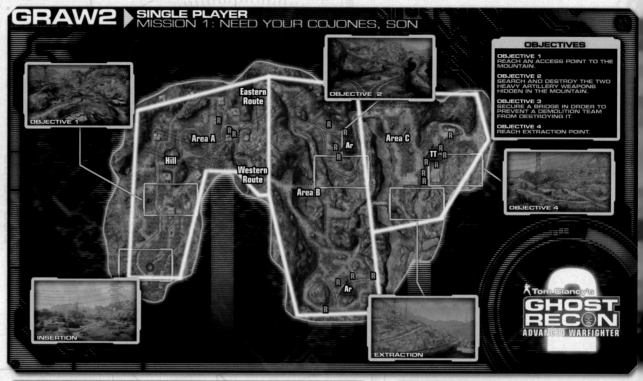

### OBJECTIVES

**OBJECTIVE 1**
REACH AN ACCESS POINT TO THE MOUNTAIN.

**OBJECTIVE 2**
SEARCH AND DESTROY THE TWO HEAVY ARTILLERY WEAPONS HIDDEN IN THE MOUNTAIN.

**OBJECTIVE 3**
SECURE A BRIDGE IN ORDER TO PREVENT A DEMOLITION TEAM FROM DESTROYING IT.

**OBJECTIVE 4**
REACH EXTRACTION POINT.

## LEGEND

- **O** = Insertion Point
- **◎** = Extraction Point
- **R** = Rifleman (Soldats)
- **TT** = Transport Truck
- **Ar** = Artillery

## OBJECTIVES

1. Get into position.
2. Search and destroy artillery pieces.
3. Secure the bridge.
4. Reach extraction point.

## MISSION BRIEFING

Your team has flown across the border into Mexico.

You've foiled a putsch in Mexico City, but the fight continues at Juarez, right on the border. Intel says the enemy may be in possession of some nasty technology. Your orders are to punch a hole through the enemy lines to Juarez and neutralize all possible dirty bombs.

## 1. GET INTO POSITION

MAP SECTION A

### Orders

Reach the area where the artillery weapons are hidden. Several approaches are possible.

**Assemble your team.**

Your first combat mission takes you into the mountains outside of Juarez. Before you can move into the Mexican border town, you must clear out enemy artillery in position to attack your forces as you move in. Your first task as the commander of the Ghosts is to pick your team for this mission. Which rifleman you choose does not really matter, but it is a good idea to go with a grenadier and a marksman for the other two slots. As for your weapons, take the Rx4 Storm. Choose whichever pistol you want, along with the defensive grenade pack.

**Move east toward the village.**

Position your team behind this wall and then help them clear the village.

Start by ordering your team to Regroup on you, and then lead them east. The southern part of the village holds three hostiles. A small hill overlooks the town from the northwest. You could move your team onto the hill, but there is not a lot of cover on it. Going around to the east does not give you a good view of the hostiles, so the best way is to stay to the south of the hill and along the western side. Set your team's ROE to Recon mode and lead them to the wall next to the westernmost building. Take up a position behind the wall to the east of your team's position. Locate all three hostiles before you begin the firefight. Change the ROE to Assault once your team is in position and then help them take out the enemies. The Rx4 rifle has a scope, so use it to engage enemies at long range.

## TIP

Even though there is not a lot of cover, the hill could be a good alternative spot from which to clear the village because you have the marksman along. Order your team to move to the southern edge of the hill and then select targets. While in Recon mode, give a Snipe order. After the first shot is taken, switch to Assault mode and help your team clear the village. You are at long range, so the enemy will rarely be able to hit your team.

**Take the path leading to the west and high ground.**

After all three hostiles have been neutralized, move south into the village. Then choose which way to enter the area containing the artillery. Since it is better to take the high ground, head up the pathway that leads west until you reach the objective location.

# 2. SEARCH AND DESTROY ARTILLERY PIECES

## MAP SECTION B

### Orders

Destroy two artillery pieces.

**Use the UAV to scout ahead for hostiles guarding the artillery.**

When you arrive at the objective location, Josh contacts you. A UAV has been assigned for you to use to locate the artillery pieces. Select it on the Cross-Com and then activate the CFV to take control of it. Move the UAV along the pathway from your location to the west to locate the first artillery unit. Locate the four hostiles in the area and then deactivate the CFV so the UAV will return to high altitude and continue to monitor the situation below.

**See what your team can see through the CFV and give them attack orders from this view as well.**

**Help your team clear the area around the artillery.**

Use the tactical map to order your team to move south and cross the wooden bridge, then to go west so they are overlooking the enemy. Meanwhile, head west along the pathway north of the bridge. Use the CFV so you can see what your team can see and order them to begin attacking the hostiles below. Move into position so you can add your fire support and clear the area. Be

sure the hostile behind the sandbags in the northwestern corner is eliminated before heading down to the artillery.

**Plant C4 on the artillery to destroy it.**

Check the area one more time with the UAV before approaching the artillery. Walk up to it and stand in front of the C4 icon, then press the action button to place the explosive charge on the artillery. Quickly move back before the timed charge detonates. Be sure your team is at a distance as well or they may be killed or wounded. One artillery piece destroyed—one more to go.

**Your team can cause a lot of damage from the position behind the crates while you attack from above.**

**Watch out for hostiles that might be hiding in the cave.**

PRIMA OFFICIAL GAME GUIDE

THE CAMPAIGN

Move into the cave to destroy the second artillery piece.

The second artillery unit is hidden in a cave to the east. Take control of the UAV and move it to this area of the battlefield to locate the four hostiles in this area. Now move your team into position. Set them to Recon mode. Order them to take the path leading down to the lower level and take cover behind some crates to the west of the cave. Then take the high path, taking cover behind a wooden fence overlooking the area. Once your team is in position, change their ROE to Assault. Snipe at enemies below to help clear the area. When it looks clear, check with the UAV and then move your team to the crates near the cave's entrance to cover it while you head down to the lower level. Enter the cave with caution in case one of the hostiles took refuge inside. Once it is clear, plant C4 on the artillery and then get out before it explodes.

# 3. Secure the Bridge

## Map Section C

### Orders

Neutralize all enemies on the bridge so the engineers can wire it to blow.

### Secondary Objective

Neutralize fleeing vehicle.

You receive new orders once both artillery pieces are destroyed. Your team must now secure the bridge. There are two ways to approach the bridge. While the eastern route leads out onto a hill overlooking the bridge area, the western route offers some crates that can be used for cover. Lead your team through a cave toward the western route and put them into Recon mode.

Scan the bridge area with the UAV.

Send your UAV ahead of you and then take control of it to scout out the enemy. You will detect several hostiles on the bridge and truck. Destroying the truck before it can flee is your secondary objective.

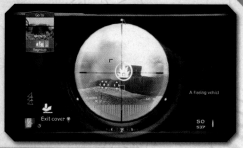

When the grenadier takes out the truck, he will usually also eliminate a few of the hostiles standing near it.

Move onto the bridge to clear off any enemies.

Move your team along the path toward the bridge and order them to take cover behind a crate. Locate the truck and order your team to attack it as you switch their ROE to Assault. Your grenadier can usually take care of the truck for you. Some of the hostiles will take a path down from the bridge and take cover in the base area below the bridge. Keep your team targeting these enemies while you head up the western path leading out onto the bridge. You can find cover behind crates on the bridge as you clear out any hostiles still on the bridge. Then you can fire down from the bridge on the enemy below or advance to the opposite end of the bridge and come down behind the hostiles to catch them in a crossfire. Once all enemies have been eliminated, this objective is complete.

# 4. Reach Extraction Point

### Orders

Move to ground transport for extraction.

Advance to the vehicle, which you take to the next mission.

The final objective is to head to the extraction point. It is at the southeastern end of the bridge. Your team automatically moves there, so all you have to worry about is getting yourself to the Humvee. Once you arrive, the mission is complete.

# Knock 'Em Dead

## GRAW2 ▶ SINGLE PLAYER
### MISSION 2: KNOCK 'EM DEAD

### OBJECTIVES

**OBJECTIVE 1**
ELIMINATE REBEL PATROL PRIOR TO RECIEVING A M.U.L.E. WITH NEW EQUIPMENT.

**OBJECTIVE 2**
RETRIEVE THE COUNTER-SNIPE RIFLE FROM THE BACK OF THE M.U.L.E.

**OBJECTIVE 3**
SECURE THE ENTRANCE OF THE REBEL CAMP SO A SUPPORT HELICOPTER CAN LAND WITH REINFORCEMENTS.

**OBJECTIVE 4**
RETRIEVE TEAMMATES WHO ARE ARRIVING IN THE BLACKHAWK.

**OBJECTIVE 5**
ELIMINATE ALL OTHER ENEMIES IN THE CAMP.

**OBJECTIVE 6**
REACH BLACKHAWK FOR EXTRACTION.

## LEGEND

- ◉ = Insertion Point
- ◎ = Extraction Point
- **Mu** = MULE
- **R** = Rifleman (Soldats)
- **G** = Machine Gunner (Soldats)
- **Mo** = Mortar (Soldats)
- **TT** = Transport Truck

## OBJECTIVES

1. Neutralize the sentries.
2. Reach the MULE to get new equipment.
3. Approach the camp entrance.
4. Neutralize enemies at camp entrance.
5. Clear the camp.
6. Reach extraction point.

## MISSION BRIEFING

**You are dropped off by yourself to start off this mission.**

After neutralizing an enemy artillery defense line, you must enter a rebel base on the way to Juarez and take it out.

## 1. NEUTRALIZE THE SENTRIES

MAP SECTION A

### Orders

You must clear the area so that you can receive support assets.

When the enemy helicopters fly over, you know that you are getting close to the enemy.

You are solo for the first part of this mission. The Humvee drops you off at an intersection of mountain roads. You get to pick your weapons for this mission. Go with the MR-C for this first part. The secondary weapon does not matter, but take along either the offensive or defensive grenade pack so you have some frag grenades as well as smoke grenades.

Kill the first two hostiles from a prone position. They will not even see you if you take them both out quickly.

Once you are loaded up, head northeast toward the objective location. As you get within about 60 meters of your objective, crouch down and proceed with caution. Four hostiles await up ahead at the small base area. As you get closer, drop prone and crawl forward until you can see the vehicle through the gap in the two large rocks. Two of the hostiles are usually near the vehicle. Use the scope to zoom in on the targets, hold your breath, let off a quick burst to take out one, and then quickly dispatch the second.

Use the cover of the stone structure while clearing out the rest of this area.

If you took out the first two hostiles quickly, the other two may not know you are there yet. Crawl up the rise to the east and take cover behind the remains of a stone structure. Glance through an opening to locate the two remaining hostiles in the base area below. Again use your scope to quickly eliminate these two enemies and secure the area.

## TIP

If you are unable to surprise the enemies and they start shooting at you before you can get behind some good cover from which you can return fire, throw a smoke grenade to create some concealment. Then you can activate your ENVG so you can see through the smoke and take out the hostiles while you move out from behind cover. Just be sure to act quickly and switch back to regular view to make sure the smoke has not dissipated or you will be an open target for the enemy.

# 2. REACH THE MULE TO GET NEW EQUIPMENT

## Orders

Learn how to use the MULE and exchange your primary weapon for a sniper rifle.

The MULE can be a great asset during a mission.

Select a sniper rifle for the next part of the mission.

Now that the area is clear, a new support asset can arrive on the scene. The MULE is a mobile supply container. Advance toward the MULE and move around to the rear of the remote vehicle to open the hatch. You will first see the News screen and can then go to the Weapons screen. You are assigned the SR A550 sniper rifle. You do not have a choice. When carrying a sniper rifle, take along a bit more firepower for your secondary weapon since sniper rifles are not as effective when fighting up close. Select an MP5 A3 submachine gun. Also take either the offensive or defensive pack of grenades again. You have also been given command of a UAV, which you can use to locate enemies and scout out the terrain ahead.

# 3. APPROACH THE CAMP ENTRANCE

MAP SECTION B

## Orders

You must advance toward the entrance of the enemy camp, neutralizing hostiles as you go.

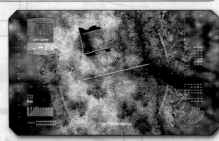

Use the UAV to locate the two hostiles, and then eliminate them.

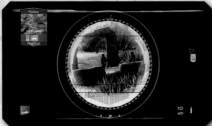

Take control of the UAV in command full view and have it scan the area ahead of you to the east. A pathway leads down to a ruined stone structure where a couple of hostiles are patrolling. Once you locate these two, exit CFV before the UAV gets shot down. Advance toward the enemies and drop prone before they are in view; crawl the rest of the way. You have two levels of zoom with your scope, so take aim, hold your breath, and drop one of the hostiles. The other may try to hide behind cover. This sniper rifle can shoot through a wall, so take aim and eliminate the second foe.

## NOTE

If you fire at a target behind a wall and the shot does not kill or even wound your foe, the enemy may actually be behind two walls—on the outside of the structure on the opposite side. Move so that you can get a shot through a window or other opening so there is only one wall between you and your target.

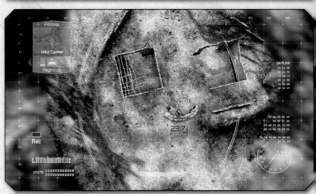

The UAV can detect the four hostiles ahead of you.

Before advancing, send the UAV to the east, taking control of it in CFV. There are three hostiles on the small hill in the center of the area and a fourth hiding in some elevated ruins at the far eastern end. Locate all four and then send the UAV to a point in the middle of these two groups so it will continue to monitor these enemies. Exit CFV.

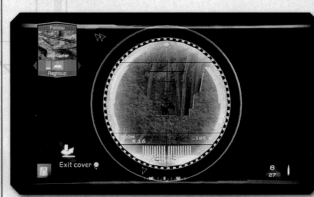

These hostiles will be firing at you, so stay behind cover, wait for them to stop firing, then quickly take aim and shoot before they have a chance to return fire. Quickly return to cover after each shot.

Rise to a crouch and move so that you have a shot at the hostile off by himself on the top of the ridge. You can shoot him without exposing yourself to the others. You can use the stone wall to the southeast of your position, near where you shot the first two hostiles with your sniper rifle, for cover. However, you must cross an opening where you will more than likely come under enemy fire. While you could stand up and run for the wall and perhaps not get hit, it is safer to create some concealment. Throw a couple of smoke grenades to mask your movement to the wall. Once the smoke has built up, run and take cover behind the wall.

With the UAV monitoring the hostiles so that the red intel markers still show up on your HUD, activate your E.N.V.G. and start taking out your three remaining targets. Remember, you can shoot right through most of the cover behind which the enemies are hiding. Once this area is clear, you can move from behind cover and bring the MULE up. You can order it to either regroup on you or to move to a position near you. Access the rear so you can stock up on some more ammo for your sniper rifle. Also take the destructive pack, which includes satchel charges, since you will have to destroy a vehicle later on in the mission. Now continue on to the objective location to enter the next area.

## TIP

If you were wounded during the engagement, you can heal yourself by resupplying from the MULE.

# 4. NEUTRALIZE ENEMIES AT CAMP ENTRANCE
## MAP SECTION C

### Orders
Before the rest of your squad can be brought in, you must clear out the camp's entrance.

### Secondary Objective
Neutralize fleeing vehicle.

You have the height advantage when sniping on the enemies guarding the entrance to the camp.

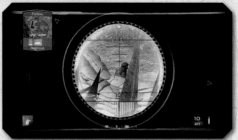

**The first hostile won't even know you are in the area.**

As before, take control of the UAV and scan the area ahead. You will detect several hostiles as well as a truck. The truck is the secondary objective. Don't worry about it for now. You must take out most of the hostiles below. Use the rocky ridges to conceal you as you pick them off one at a time, beginning with the western-most target—the one to your right—and working your way east. Because of the distance, the enemy should not see you. If necessary to make a shot, move forward and take cover behind the stone wall.

The satchel charge in the road is a great way to destroy the truck.

**Your team arrives to help you with the next objective.**

After you kill several hostiles, some of the remaining run away. Try to get a few if you can, but don't spend too much time on them. As they start to flee, so does the truck. It drives slowly toward the western exit from the area. Quickly run down the pathway and throw a satchel charge into the road. Back away, wait for the truck to drive near it, and then detonate the charge. The truck explodes and you have completed the secondary objective. Head back up the path to where a Blackhawk is dropping off the rest of your squad.

## TIP

The SR A550 sniper rifle can also be used against vehicles. Shoot at the truck if you don't have a satchel charge or want to try an

alternative way of destroying it. You have to get a lot of hits to destroy it, so start attacking the truck before it begins to move or right at the start of its movement. The intel display on your HUD shows the damage you inflict as its "health" percentage decreases with each hit.

# 5. CLEAR THE CAMP

### MAP SECTION D

## Orders

Eliminate all enemies within the camp.

**Move quickly—the enemy fires mortars at you.**

When you reach the Blackhawk, you can select your team. Take along any of the riflemen for the first slot, the gunner for the second slot, and another rifleman for the third slot. You want your squad to have a lot of firepower for a medium-range fight as you move in on the camp. As for yourself, try out the SCAR-H assault rifle. Also take along a pistol and either the offensive or defensive grenade pack since both types of grenades can come in handy.

**Some hostiles are waiting for you near the entrance. Take them out as you advance.**

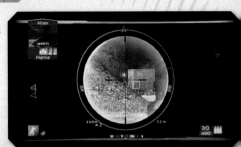

**Get to this tunnel, which is the entrance to the camp.**

Once your team is ready, start moving. The enemy in the camp is firing mortars at your team, so head toward the camp entrance to the south. You can see the mortar rounds coming in, so try to stay away from them. You can head along either the eastern or western side as you advance on the tunnel leading to the camp. As you approach the tunnel, be ready for a couple of hostiles that take cover behind some crates. Take them out on the move—you don't have time to stop and use cover. Keep your teammates moving along with you so they don't get hit by a mortar round. If you want your team to help you take out the two hostiles, be sure to switch the ROE to Assault mode. Then change it back to Recon once the enemies are dead.

**Order your team to take cover behind these crates.**

At the tunnel, take cover behind the first set of crates on the right along with your team. Once in the tunnel, you don't have to worry about the mortar anymore. Hopefully the enemy has not spotted your team as you moved into position. Take control of the UAV and bring it in over the camp to locate all of the hostiles inside, and then exit CFV so the UAV will return to a higher altitude in the middle of the camp and continue to monitor the movements of the hostiles below.

**Take cover behind these crates as you engage the enemies in the camp.**

When you are ready to start the attack, throw a smoke grenade out to cover the front of the tunnel and send your team to the crate ahead on the left while you move to the crates outside of the tunnel on the right. The smoke will conceal your team as you move into position and allow you to take out a few hostiles before they can see to return fire. From these positions, you should be able to eliminate all of the enemies. However, if necessary, move yourself or your team to the right of your position to try to flank the hostiles.

## NOTE

An M50 fixed machine gun is behind some sandbags to the south of the tunnel entrance of the camp. You can man it and use it to engage the enemy. The downside is that you will be exposed to enemy fire. It is better to stay behind cover and use your assault rifle. However, once you have eliminated most of the enemies, try using it to finish off the last one or two targets.

# 6. REACH THE EXTRACTION POINT

Lead your team out of the camp for a ride to the next mission.

**Your ride is here.**

After you have cleared out the enemy camp, all that remains is to extract your team. Order your team to regroup on you and then lead it back out through the tunnel to the objective location. A Blackhawk is inbound to pick you up for your next mission.

# Unpleasant Surprise

**OBJECTIVES**

1. Clear the bridge.
2. Clear the enemy base.
3. Neutralize rebel weapon convoy.

## Mission Briefing

**Your feet get a rest while you ride through this mission.**

A weapon resupply convoy heading for Juarez has managed to escape from the camp. You need to neutralize it before those weapons are delivered.

## 1. Clear the Bridge

**You are coming down on the bridge.**

This mission takes place while you man an M134 chain gun mounted on a Blackhawk. The pilot will fly you to different areas on the battlefield and then orbit around allowing you to eliminate enemies as you go. The trucks of the convoy are your main targets. You must also engage and destroy other vehicles and infantry that fire on your helicopter.

**Destroying the trucks will get rid of most of the infantry.**

**TIP**

The chain gun takes a second or two to start spinning before it will fire, so you have to pull the trigger before you want to start hitting the target. Because of this delay, it is best to keep the chain gun firing for long bursts.

Your first area is the bridge that you cleared during a previous mission. U.S. engineers mined the bridge, and a convoy of weapons trucks is now stuck there. As the Blackhawk flies in, start shooting at the enemies below. Target the trucks first since they will explode when destroyed and kill nearby infantry. Once the three trucks are eliminated, mop up any remaining infantry.

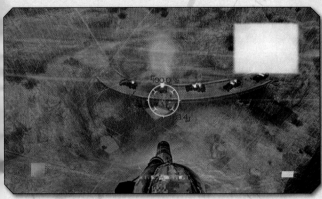
Make sure nothing is left when you fly away from the bridge.

## NOTE

The gauge in the bottom-right corner of the screen is the chain gun's heat meter. The longer you fire, the shorter this meter becomes, changing from green to yellow and finally to red to represent the gun overheating. Lay off the trigger occasionally when there are no targets right in front of you to allow the gun to cool down.

## 2. CLEAR THE ENEMY BASE

The base is filled with infantry.

Take out those fixed machine guns.

Once the bridge is cleared, your pilot takes you to the enemy base. Here you have to fire on lots of infantry. As you make the first pass, go after the fixed machine gun emplacements, which are behind sandbags, since they represent the biggest threat. A good tactic is to get the elevation of your gun just right and then fire away, letting the motion of the helicopter bring targets into your sights.

The anti-tank gunner appears at this spot. Kill him quickly.

The Blackhawk will come in low so you can get a better shot at the hostiles on the ground.

As the Blackhawk begins to turn at the end of the first run and passes by the water tower, watch for an anti-tank soldier below that will fire a rocket at your helicopter. He is your primary target now since his weapon can cause a lot of damage to your ride. After making a pass down the opposite side of the base, the pilot takes you down the middle. Continue to mow down infantry to clear the base.

# 3. NEUTRALIZE REBEL WEAPON CONVOY

The trucks are escorted by armored cars.

Destroy anything that moves at the tunnel exit to prevent these weapons and troops from reaching Juarez.

Be sure to destroy all of the trucks, even as your Blackhawk pulls ahead of them.

A convoy of vehicles begins to flee from the base as you are making your runs. The pilot takes the Blackhawk on a course parallel to the road. In addition to the trucks you must destroy, the enemy convoy contains armored cars, which will fire on your helicopter. Blast them as well. The armored cars are a bit tougher to destroy due to their added protection and the erratic way they are driven.

The convoy eventually reaches a tunnel, preventing you from continuing your attack. Don't worry. The pilot takes you around to the other side of the tunnel, where you can wait for the remaining vehicles. The enemy has set up some defenses at the end of the tunnel, so when you arrive, take out the infantry to keep it from firing on your Blackhawk. Keep an eye on the tunnel and destroy any vehicles as they emerge. Once all of the enemies here have been eliminated, the mission is complete.

THE CAMPAIGN

# This Place Is an Inferno

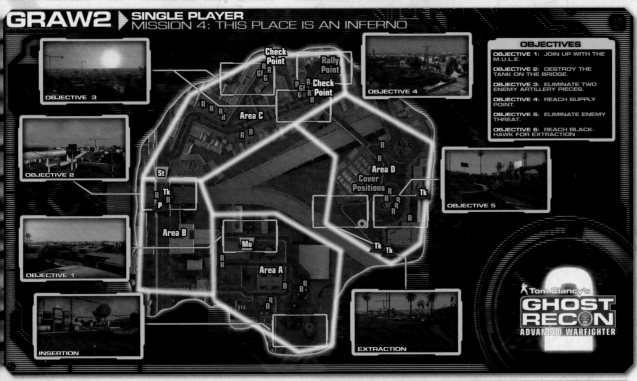

**OBJECTIVES**

OBJECTIVE 1: JOIN UP WITH THE M.U.L.E.

OBJECTIVE 2: DESTROY THE TANK ON THE BRIDGE.

OBJECTIVE 3: ELIMINATE TWO ENEMY ARTILLERY PIECES.

OBJECTIVE 4: REACH SUPPLY POINT.

OBJECTIVE 5: ELIMINATE ENEMY THREAT.

OBJECTIVE 6: REACH BLACK-HAWK FOR EXTRACTION

## LEGEND

- ◎ = Insertion Point
- ◎ = Extraction Point
- **Mu** = MULE
- **St** = Striker
- **R** = Rifleman (Soldats)
- **G** = Machine Gunner (Soldats)
- **Gf** = Machine Gun Fixed (Soldats)
- **Tk** = Tank (Soldats)
- **P** = Panhard (Soldats)

## OBJECTIVES

1. Help loyalists.
2. Destroy the tank.
3. Clear the rebel checkpoints.
4. Move to rally point.
5. Neutralize all hostiles.
6. Reach extraction point.

## MISSION BRIEFING

**Your team is moving into Juarez, finally.**

Thanks to you, the road is now open to Juarez. Your mission is to enter the city with the help of the loyal Mexican soldiers and, once inside, locate and neutralize all potential NBC (nuclear, biological, chemical) threats.

## 1. HELP LOYALISTS

MAP SECTION A

### Orders

Reach the MULE to get new equipment.

**You start off with a fight as soon as the mission begins.**

The mission begins with your team set down near a firefight between the loyal Mexican troops and the rebels. When selecting your team, take along a rifleman from the first slot, a grenadier from the second slot, and another rifleman from the third slot. As for yourself, the Rx4 Storm assault rifle is a good choice, along with a pistol and the defensive pack of grenades.

Send your team across this road while you engage the enemies at the western end.

**Put your team behind cover.**

Once the area is clear, order your team to regroup on you, then head north toward the location of the MULE. When you come to a road, take cover along the side of a building and peek around the corner to look for hostiles to the west. There are a couple at the end of the road. Order your team to move across the road to a position behind cover while you take aim down the road and engage any enemies that may try to fire on you or your team. Hold these positions until you kill both enemies.

**Help your team clear out the hostiles.**

Upon disembarking from the Blackhawk, lead your team through the open gates of the chain-link fence to take cover behind stacks of lumber. Hostiles will appear to the north and northeast, so be ready for them and set your team's ROE to Assault mode. Help your teammates take down the hostiles. As they maneuver around behind cover, you may need to order them to shift position in order to get the shots. Don't forget to give orders to target specific enemies so your teammates will concentrate fire on individual hostiles.

**Access the MULE for an anti-tank weapon.**

Now that the road is clear, move quickly to the MULE and pick up the Zeus T2 anti-tank weapon. Take along an MP5 A3 submachine gun for your secondary weapon and a defensive pack of grenades.

# 2. DESTROY THE TANK

## Orders

Destroy enemy tank with the Zeus T2.

## Secondary Objective

Neutralize fleeing vehicle.

The tank is bombarding the Mexican Army troops. Help them out.

The Mexican troops are taking a pounding from a rebel tank. It is up to you to take it out. You must do this on your own, so leave your teammates behind or they may get killed or wounded by the tank. Head west toward the north-south road that leads across the river. The tank is positioned on the bridge. Take cover behind a building to the south of the bridge. From there you can see the tank and a Panhard armored car. The Panhard is your secondary objective. Since it will flee if you don't act fast, take it out first.

From this corner, you can see both vehicles.

Keep the tank centered in your sights as the missile flies toward its target.

The Zeus T2 is a radio-controlled missile. Once you fire it, keep the target in your sights and the missile will score a hit. This allows you to hit moving targets with greater accuracy. The launcher has a scope view; however, at this range you can still get a hit without it. Aim at the Panhard and fire. One hit is all it takes to destroy this vehicle. Step back behind cover while you reload the launcher and then target the M1A1 tank. The tank is much tougher, requiring two hits to destroy. After getting the first hit, move behind cover to reload, then fire again. Don't waste too much time or the tank will start moving toward you and firing on your position.

# 3. CLEAR THE REBEL CHECKPOINTS

## Orders

Clear the two rebel checkpoints.

This Stryker is yours to command for this part of the mission.

The bridge is now secure, so bring your team and the MULE to your position. Reload your supply of missiles. Switch to your submachine gun since you will be facing enemy infantry during this next phase of the mission. Order your team to regroup on you and move across the bridge.

A Mexican Army Stryker APC has been assigned to you for this phase. Use it to help you clear out the two checkpoints. You can give the Stryker basic orders. If you look at the tactical map, you will see a green path down the roads that the Stryker will follow. The Stryker can be ordered to move forward and move back along the path, or to stop. You can also see what it sees via CFV and even give it Attack orders.

Head into town and lead your team to take cover by this wall.

Continue down the alley to engage the enemy across the street.

Lead your team down the street and order it to take cover along the wall with the "Hot Bar" neon sign. A couple of hostiles come around the corner. Take them out. Move the Stryker forward to your location. Lead your team east down the alley to a position from which you can cover the road to the north. Then order the Stryker to move forward until it turns the corner and is facing east. Between the Stryker and your team, you can clear out the enemies along the road and the sniper on the rooftop to the east. Use the CFV on the Stryker to select targets, and take out enemies on your own with your submachine gun.

Bring the Stryker forward and use the CFV to give it Attack orders.

Now go after the first checkpoint. Send your team across the road to take cover behind a wall on the western side. Set ROE to Recon mode so your team can locate the enemies at the checkpoint at the end of the road. A fixed machine gun and other soldiers await behind sandbags. Switch to Assault mode and bring the Stryker forward until it makes the turn and is facing the checkpoint. You can use the Zeus T2 to fire on the enemy as well. Aim for the sandbags or the truck behind the hostiles so that the explosion will kill the infantry.

Set up your team to fire on the checkpoint form the side.

Flank the second checkpoint and hit it from behind.

Advance down the road to the location of the first checkpoint once it is clear and approach the second checkpoint from the north. Position your teammates along a wall near the burned out car and keep them on Assault. Meanwhile, run east across the road and enter an alley that allows you to come in behind the enemy checkpoint. Move the Stryker forward to keep the enemies focused away from you so you can clear them out.

# 4. MOVE TO RALLY POINT

## Orders

Lead your team to the rally point for resupply.

Swap out team-mates as well as weapons at the rally point.

The Blackhawk has touched down to the east. Lead your team to it to prepare for the next phase of the mission. If some of your riflemen are wounded, swap them out for other teammates. You need a rifleman, a grenadier, and, most important, an anti-tank gunner, since you will have some tanks to deal with before the mission is over. You need this soldier because you can't carry the Zeus for the rest of the mission. However, you now have access to the MK48 LMG. You will face lots of infantry, so your job is to lay down suppressing fire for your soldiers while they engage individual hostiles.

# 5. NEUTRALIZE ALL HOSTILES

### MAP SECTION D

## Orders

Neutralize all hostiles around the market.

Use the cars for cover as you move across the bridge.

Your team is now loaded for bear. Lead it toward the bridge to the southeast and order it to take cover behind a wall to the right side of the bridge. The Mexican Army is engaged to the east, so you can ignore the action and explosions in that direction. Move out onto the bridge and use the cars for cover. Send your team to take cover behind another car farther ahead. When it's in position to cover you, move ahead yourself. You run into a couple of hostiles along the way, so take them down. Make sure your team is set for Assault.

**Your team moves to cover behind the planter.**

As you approach the open-air market off to the right, order your team to a position behind a planter while you move into the market and continue to the southern side to find a couple of concrete walls you can use for cover. Take position behind the one on the left and send your team to the one on the right.

**Move into the market area.**

Set your team up behind this wall in the market.

Hostiles move toward you from the south. They use barricades for cover. After your team is in position, drop prone and crawl around to the right toward the stairs. There is another concrete wall on the side of the stairs that you can hide behind as well as a gap through which you can fire. Light machine guns are more accurate when fired from the prone position, and if you stay to the left of the gap, you can engage and take out several of the enemies as they move forward to fire at your team.

Order your team to engage this tank. You can also order them to attack using the tactical map so you don't have to expose yourself to enemy fire.

Air support takes care of another one.

As you kill the enemies, a rebel tank shows up. Order your team to target it either by aiming at it with your reticle or using the tactical map. Your anti-tank gunner fires a couple of missiles into the tank to destroy it. However, a couple more tanks are on

their way from the southeast. Luckily, you have been given some air support—just in time. To call in an air strike on the tanks, select the air support on the Cross-Com and then target one of the tanks. Switch to your team and order it to engage the other tank. Meanwhile, you can fire at any remaining infantry. Between the air strike and your team, the tanks don't stand a chance. Finish off any remaining hostiles to complete this objective.

The area is clear.

# 6. REACH EXTRACTION POINT

## Orders

Lead your team to the landing zone for extraction.

Get back to the Black-hawk once the mission is complete.

This last firefight can be deadly. If any of your teammates are down, quickly heal them before they die. Your mission is complete. Now all you have to do is get to the Blackhawk, which lands to the southwest. As your team flies away from the scene, a large explosion erupts from the market. High levels of radiation are detected. The rebels must have been storing a nuclear device in the area. Things have just gotten a lot hotter.

The Rebels have blown the market—and radiation is being detected!

THE CAMPAIGN

# You'll Be Inserted Solo

## GRAW2 ▶ SINGLE PLAYER
### MISSION 5: YOU'LL BE INSERTED SOLO

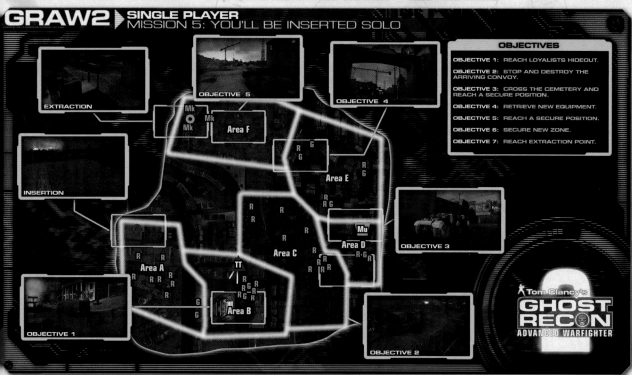

### OBJECTIVES

**OBJECTIVE 1:** REACH LOYALISTS HIDEOUT.

**OBJECTIVE 2:** STOP AND DESTROY THE ARRIVING CONVOY.

**OBJECTIVE 3:** CROSS THE CEMETERY AND REACH A SECURE POSITION.

**OBJECTIVE 4:** RETRIEVE NEW EQUIPMENT.

**OBJECTIVE 5:** REACH A SECURE POSITION.

**OBJECTIVE 6:** SECURE NEW ZONE.

**OBJECTIVE 7:** REACH EXTRACTION POINT.

## LEGEND

- ◉ = Insertion Point
- ◎ = Extraction Point
- **Mu** = MULE
- **R** = Rifleman (Soldats)
- **G** = Machine Gunner (Soldats)
- **Mk** = Marksman (Soldats)
- **TT** = Transport Truck

## OBJECTIVES

1. Reach rendezvous point.
2. Neutralize enemy reinforcements.
3. Move to cemetery exit.
4. Reach the MULE.
5. Reach fallback position.
6. Neutralize snipers.
7. Reach extraction point.

## MISSION BRIEFING

CIUDAD JUAREZ
PANTEON TEPEYAC          02:09:28

**The Blackhawk lands you on a rooftop to start this mission.**

The enemy has used a nuclear device to stop the loyal soldiers, and the U.S. Army is unjustly accused of peacekeepers' deaths. It's impossible to risk a direct assault. You'll be inserted in Juarez and will rendezvous with friendlies who will help you find the nukes.

## 1. REACH RENDEZVOUS POINT

### MAP SECTION A

### Orders

Reach the rendezvous point near the cemetery to link up with loyal Mexican forces.

This entire mission requires you to go solo. Though you are alone, you have several things going for you. First, it is night, and while you can see through the darkness with your ENVG, the rebels cannot. Furthermore, you have access to the MR-C guncam, which allows you to fire around or over cover without exposing your body. The camera built into the weapons sight will display the view onto your monocle. Be sure to take the MR-C LW SD rifle for this mission along with the MP5A3 SD submachine gun with a silencer. This gives you some additional firepower if you run out of ammo for your primar̶̶̶n. You also need the destructive pack so you can take out ̶̶̶̶ks later in the mission.

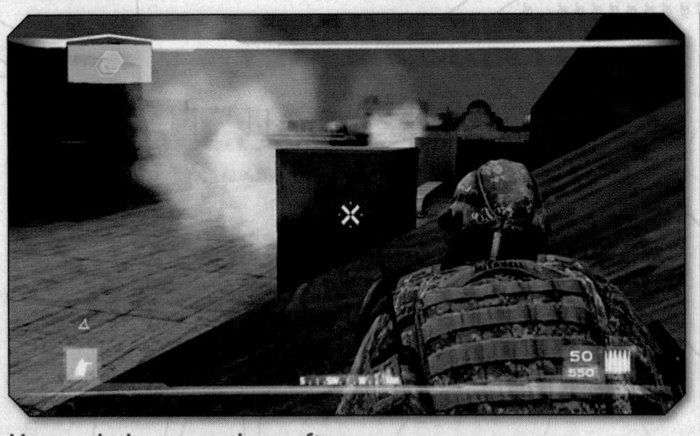

**Move quietly across the rooftops.**

The Blackhawk inserts you onto a rooftop. You must make your way across several rooftops, clearing them of hostiles before you reach the street level. While you have to make lots of twists and turns, this part of the mission is linear—you can only go one way. The key is to stay low and go slow. By moving crouched, you make less noise. Eight hostiles dot the rooftops, and another two await on the streets below.

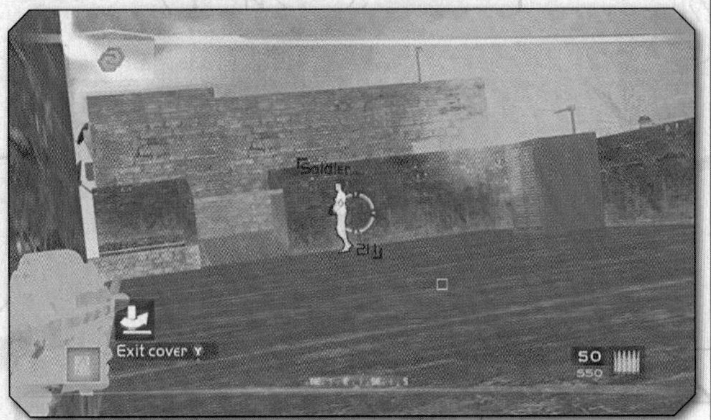


**Use the guncam feature and ENVG to take out enemies in the dark without exposing yourself.**

From the landing zone, head south down the stairs, then move west before turning south again. Take cover against the wall on your left side and edge toward the corner to locate the hostile to the east. Use your ENVG. These goggles not only amplify what little light there is, they also show heat sources so that the warm bodies of the hostiles stand out. As you move past the corner of the cover, instead of peeking around, stick your guncam out. Use aim mode for close shots and the scope/camera for longer shots. The MR-C LW SD only has a fully automatic rate of fire, so to conserve ammo and increase accuracy, fire it in short bursts. Unless you get a head shot, it will take a few rounds to kill an enemy. Kill this first hostile without exposing yourself.

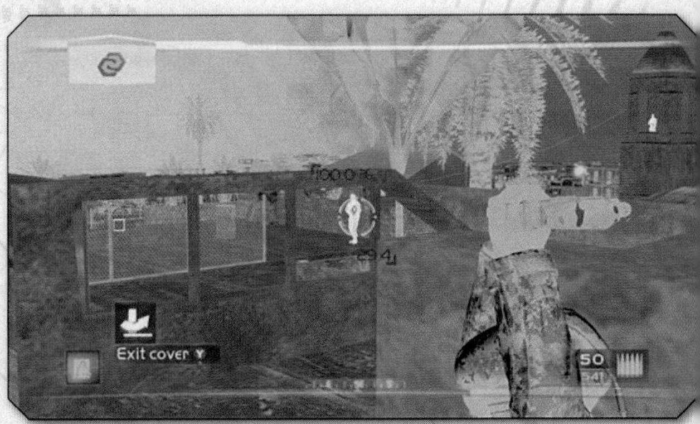


**After taking out this hostile, be sure to get the one in the tower.**

Continue east until you come to some stairs leading down to the right. A hostile lurks on the lower roof to the southeast. Take cover against the low wall and raise your gun above the wall to take him out. Another hostile hides in the tower to the south, so be sure to kill him before you head down the stairs or he will cause you some pain.

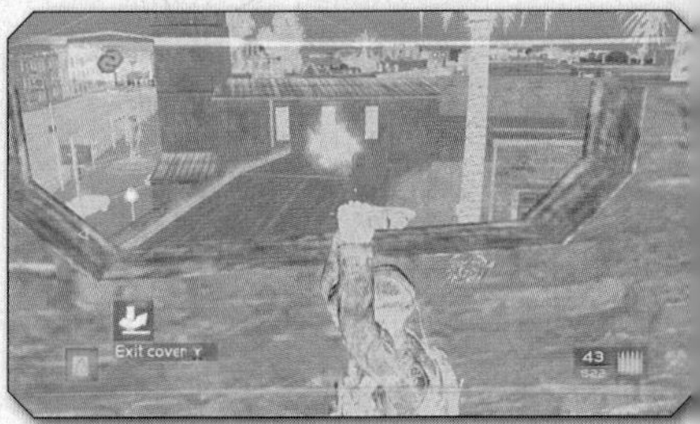

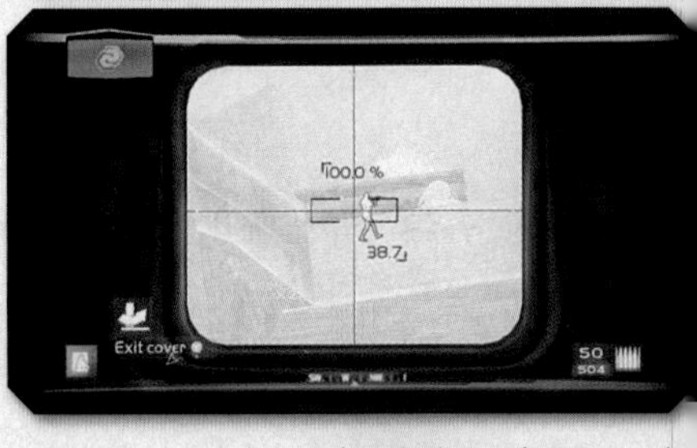

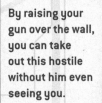

**By raising your gun over the wall, you can take out this hostile without him even seeing you.**

After clearing this area, descend the stairs and continue south to the wall at the roof's edge. From here you can take out another enemy below and to the south. Now head down the ramp to the north and continue around to the south to the place where the last enemy you killed was patrolling. As you start to go up another ramp, take cover against the wall to the right and raise your gun over the top to locate and kill a couple more patrolling hostiles to the southwest.

This is the last hostile on the rooftops.

As you make your way west, watch for a patrolling enemy on the higher level at the western end. Take cover behind one of the objects on the rooftop and wait for a good shot. The last hostile on the rooftops is to the southeast. He is at the far end, so you can advance about halfway and take cover behind a low wall, then shoot over it to eliminate him.

Kill the hostiles down on the street while you are still up on the rooftop.

Before heading down the ramp leading out onto the street, move to the eastern edge of the rooftop and raise your rifle over the edge to locate the two hostiles walking along the street. Use the scope view to take them out. Remember to hold your breath. There is no one else around, so if a car alarm goes off when you hit a vehicle, don't worry.

Use this building for cover.

Head down to the street and continue southeast toward the large building. Make your way toward the objective location by moving along the sidewalk south of the large building and then crossing the street to take cover on the south side of the building with the "La Chiquitita" sign.

# 2. NEUTRALIZE ENEMY REINFORCEMENTS

## MAP SECTION B

### Orders

Neutralize the reinforcements the enemy has sent to this area to stop you.

### Secondary Objective

Neutralize fleeing vehicles.

Blow up the trucks with satchel charges.

The friendlies you were expecting to meet up with are not where they are supposed to be. Instead, two truckloads of rebels have been dropped off north of your position. They will be heading south down the road, right past you. Throw a satchel out in the road and detonate it as the first truck drives near it. This causes the second truck to slow down, giving you time to throw another satchel out in front of it and detonate it.

## NOTE

You have to be looking in the direction of a satchel charge to detonate it. If the icon is yellow, you are good to go.

**Using the guncam, take out a few hostiles from the southern corner of the building. Then move around behind the building to hit the enemy from the side.**

By taking out the trucks, you have alerted the hostile infantry to your position. Head back to the building and take cover. You can kill a few from this position. However, you can get a better shot if you move east and then north along the back side of the building to hit them from the east. Since you took satchel charges, you do not have any smoke grenades to use for concealment. However, throw a frag and wait for it to detonate if you want to move past the opening in the northern part of this row of buildings. The explosion will at least cause the hostiles to take cover. Once at the building's northern corner, you can hit the enemies from the side. Move west as necessary to finish them off.

# 3. MOVE TO CEMETERY EXIT

### MAP SECTION C

### Orders

Move through the cemetery to reach the exit.

**You can kill a few hostiles in the lower cemetery from behind this wall.**

The loyal Mexican soldiers have had to move to another location, so you must make your way through more of Juarez to get to them. For this phase, you must advance through a cemetery. Head northeast from your position to the gate leading into the cemetery. As you follow the pathway to the northwest, take some time to raise your rifle over the wall on your right side to locate and kill a couple of hostiles out in the lower part of the cemetery. The more you kill now, the fewer you have to deal with later.

Continue northwest to the upper part of the cemetery. Take cover behind a wall in the southern part of this area so you can take out one of the two hostiles patrolling this area. Advance north carefully, using the monuments for cover until you can kill the second enemy. Now head east and down the stairs to the lower part of the cemetery.

**Use the monuments and walls for cover while in the cemetery.**

Even though you took out a couple of the patrolling hostiles in the lower cemetery, more await. The best tactic is to work your way to the eastern wall of the cemetery. As you move, take cover behind objects and watch for hostiles to the south. Take out any that come into your sights. Once you get to the east, slowly make your way south watching for hostiles to the south and west. The section of monuments surrounded by a short wall is a great place to hold out for a bit as you wait for some of the enemy to come to you. Keep moving south until you come to the stairs that exit the cemetery and lead to the objective location.

**Descend the stairs to get to the objective location.**

# 4. REACH THE MULE

## Orders

Reach the MULE to resupply and get new equipment.

Once you exit the cemetery, you gain some support in the form of a UAV. It will come in real handy for the rest of the mission. Use it to scout out your path to the MULE. To the northeast of your position, the UAV detects three hostiles. Deactivate CFV so the UAV will climb to a higher altitude and monitor these enemies while you move in for the kill.

can the area and then clear out these three hostiles so you can get to the MULE.

Approach them from the southwest, using the building for cover. Stick your rifle out around the corner and take out the hostiles one at a time, starting with the one to the east and working your way west. With these out of the way, it is a clear walk to the MULE. Send the UAV there ahead of you. Reach the MULE to complete this objective.

# 5. REACH FALLBACK POSITION

## Orders

Move through part of Juarez to get to the fallback position at the construction site.

**The MULE allows you to pick up a sniper rifle.**

**The UAV can detect the enemies and then monitor them while you move in for the kill.**

At the MULE, pick up a sniper rifle and heal any wounds you may have received. Try out the new DSR-1 and take along a P90SD submachine gun and a defensive pack of grenades. This section of Juarez contains eight hostiles, in three different groups—one to the west of your location, one to the north, and the third by the objective location. You do not need to take out all three groups. In fact, if you head north from your position, you can bypass the western group altogether. It is getting lighter as morning approaches; you no longer have the darkness as your ally, so use caution.

## TIP

Keep the MULE close at hand, but out of danger, as you move through this area. If you need to swap out the sniper rifle for an assault rifle, you can just visit the MULE and make the exchange; however, you can get through here with just the sniper rifle just fine.

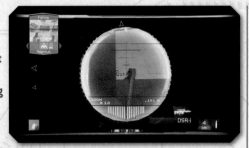

This gunner will chew you up if you don't take him out before moving to rooftops to the north.

Before moving, use the UAV to reconnoiter this area. Locate all three groups so you know where they are, then have the UAV hover over the group to the north of you so it will monitor their movements as you engage them. Head north until you can see the hostile gunner on the rooftop. Take him out. Another hostile usually runs up to the rooftop once the first one is killed. Keep moving north until you can eliminate this hostile as well.

Head up these stairs and go all the way to the rooftop to snipe at the enemies near the objective location.

Hit the third hostile from street level.

It is now time to get on a rooftop yourself. The building at the end of the road leading southeast from the group by the objective location is great. Be sure to send the UAV to detect and monitor these hostiles for you. From here you can take out at least two of that group. If you can't get the third, head down to the street level and move north a bit before turning west so that you can

approach the last hostile from the north and kill him. Continue to the objective location and bring the MULE up to reload your supply of sniper rifle ammo.

# 6. NEUTRALIZE SNIPERS

## MAP SECTION F

### Orders

Neutralize the enemy snipers on the rooftops overlooking the construction area.

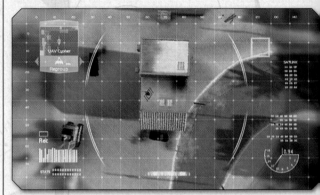

It is vital that you locate the snipers in advance.

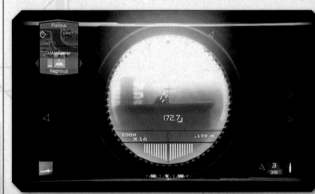

The enemy snipers are usually prone and at a range of over 170 meters.

This part of the mission is a sniper fight between you and three hostile snipers. They snipe from rooftops to the west of your position. The key is to take aim and shoot each quickly before they can shoot you. Also be sure you never expose yourself to more than one enemy sniper at a time or you will be dead. They are expecting you. Use the UAV to locate all three snipers and then position it in the middle of the three to monitor them.

There are two groups of buildings you can use for sniping. Use the southern group first and ascend the northern stairs so you have a stone wall for cover. Since the UAV is monitoring the snipers, you can see their locations on your HUD. Take up a crouched position to the left of the window and quickly peek around the corner to fire at the central sniper. Act fast or he will kill you. Quickly duck back in after the shot, reload, and go after the sniper on the left.

Climb to the top of this northern group of buildings to get a shot at the third sniper.

You can't hit the third sniper from this position. Head back down the stairs and move to the northern group of buildings. Take the stairs all the way to the top and quickly move to cover. Once again, you must quickly acquire and kill your target before he can shoot you.

# 7. REACH EXTRACTION POINT

## Orders

Meet up with the loyal Mexican soldiers at the extraction point.

Head west across the construction site.

This Humvee is waiting for you at the extraction point.

With the enemy snipers dead, you can safely make your way to the extraction point. A Mexican soldier in a Humvee is waiting to pick you up and take you to your next mission.

# The Price of Peace

## GRAW2 ▶ SINGLE PLAYER
### MISSION 6: THE PRICE OF PEACE

### OBJECTIVES

**OBJECTIVE 1**
REACH SUPPLY POINT AND JOIN SECOND SQUAD.

**OBJECTIVE 2**
DESTROY ANTI-AIRCRAFT DEFENSES.

**OBJECTIVE 3**
REACH NEXT POSITION.

**OBJECTIVE 4**
HOLD POSITION.

**OBJECTIVE 5**
REACH EXTRACTION POINT.

**OBJECTIVE 6**
HOLD POSITION UNTIL BLACKHAWK ARRIVES FOR EXTRACTION.

## LEGEND

- ◉ = Insertion Point
- ◎ = Extraction Point
- **Gt** = Ghost Truck
- **R** = Rifleman (Soldats)
- **Tk** = Tank (Soldats)
- **Ad** = Adats (Soldats)
- **P** = Panhard (Soldats)

## OBJECTIVES

1. Move to the rally point.
2. Extract the journalist.
3. Move to the rally point.
4. Hold position until extraction.
5. Reach the extraction point.
6. Extract with the Humvee.

## MISSION BRIEFING

CIUDAD JUAREZ
MISSION GUADALUPE
08:32:44

You must fight your way through war-torn Juarez to complete your objectives.

You're now inside Juarez, behind the enemy lines. Your mission is to help the loyal soldiers extract a Mexican journalist with access to the rebels who want to provide us with information.

## 1. MOVE TO THE RALLY POINT

### MAP SECTION A

### Orders

Lead a team of loyalist soldiers to get to the rally point.

You have a team of Mexican Army riflemen assigned to you for this mission.

**Head up these stairs to the rooftop.**

You have not been able to meet up with the rest of the Ghost squad yet. However, the Mexican Army commander has assigned a team of his soldiers to assist you—riflemen Diego Jimenez and Jose Gutierrez. They will follow orders just like your Ghost team, so put them to work for you. Enemy troops are headed your way from the north, so quickly order your team to take up a position behind one of the concrete barricades while you head up to the rooftop of the building to the east of your starting position.

## NOTE

Since you have not had a chance to resupply, you still have the same weapon from the last mission—a sniper rifle. This is actually the perfect weapon for this first part of the mission since your rifle can take out enemies even if they are hiding behind cover. The Mexican Army has kindly provided a full loadout of ammunition.

**Watch out for this hostile on the rooftop.**

The rooftop gives you a great field of fire across the area below.

Once at the rooftop, move to the northeast corner and take cover behind the wall. From the rooftop you have a great view of the town square below as the hostiles move in. Order your men to Assault mode so they will engage the enemy on their own. Watch out for the enemy on the rooftop to the northwest. Kill him and then pick off hostiles in the square. Keep going until the area is clear.

**Head north through this square.**

## TIP

The wall on the rooftop has some gaps in it. Lie prone on the roof and fire down on the enemies through these gaps.

**Position your team at this corner in preparation for the next attack.**

Once all hostiles have been eliminated, head back down to the street level, place your team in Recon mode, and move out toward the rally point to the north. When you get to the T intersection where you turn to the east to continue to the rally point, order your men to take cover behind the wall of the building to the west. They can then cover the area to the west later when hostiles arrive on the scene. Make your way to the rally point, where a truck carrying the Ghost squad waits for you.

# 2. Extract the Journalist

## Map Section B

### Orders

Destroy three anti-aircraft vehicles so that a helicopter can fly in to extract the journalist.

A team of Ghosts accompanies you for the rest of the mission. Since you still have the Mexican Army team, take along a rifleman, the grenadier, and the combat medic. You have a lot of close firefights ahead, and the medic can really come in handy. For yourself, take along the Rx4 Storm assault rifle, a secondary weapon of your choice, and the offensive pack of grenades.

**Engage the hostiles that come at you from two directions.**

As soon as you are back into the mission, hostiles start attacking from the west, near where you left your Mexican soldiers, and from the north. Order the Ghost team to take cover and begin engaging the enemies to the north, and change the ROE of both teams to Assault mode. Help defeat these enemies by assigning targets and adding your direct fire to the fight.

It is tough to detect hostiles in the bombed-out buildings until you are close. Therefore, be ready to fire in case you run into an enemy.

Your first objective for this part of the mission is to destroy the eastern AA vehicle. To get to it, you must advance through a bombed-out section of the town along the eastern edge. There are three pairs of hostiles in each of the three blocks between you and the AA vehicle. Due to the nature of the urban terrain, most of the fighting will be at fairly close range.

**Move your teams from cover to cover as you clear out the eastern part of the map.**

A good tactic is to send your teams ahead of you. Keep them in Recon mode so you can get as much intel as possible on the enemy positions before you engage. Once the enemy has been found, switch your teams to Assault mode, and if they can't take out the hostiles, move around to the east to try to hit the enemies from their flanks or rear. Be sure to clear out each of the three sections so that hostiles you bypassed do not come at your teams and hit you from the rear.

## NOTE

It can get confusing at first with two teams of infantry under your control. To determine which team you currently have on the Cross-Com, look at the icon. The Ghost team has three soldiers on its icon, while the Mexican Army team has only two soldiers on its icon.

One AA vehicle eliminated.

Four more hostiles guard the AA vehicle. Put your teams in Recon mode again before moving them toward the block where the objective is so they can gather intel on the location of the hostiles. If they take fire, switch them to Assault mode and move them into flanking positions to clear out this block. When it is clear, order your teams to take positions covering the road to the west of the AA vehicle while you place a C4 charge on it and blow it up.

## TIP

The combat medic can be a useful teammate during this mission. Normally the soldiers in your team can't be healed unless they  are incapacitated. However, the combat medic can bring them up to full health even if they have only taken a bit of damage. More importantly, the combat medic is the only teammate that can heal you. Since you brought him along, be sure to take advantage of his expertise to keep your team in top shape throughout this part of the mission.

Move your teams to cover behind the concrete walls to the south of the arena.

Order your team, which includes the grenadier, to to take out the Panhard armored car.

The other two AA vehicles are to the west on the other side of the bull fighting arena. To get there, you need to move across a parking lot. Order your teams to take cover behind concrete barriers along the eastern end of the parking lot. A Panhard armored car patrols the area. Order both of your teams to attack it. Shoot the gunner on top of the Panhard with your rifle, and your grenadier can destroy the vehicle itself. Advance in rushes across the parking lot, ordering your teams to use the cars for cover. Even though it looks clear, there can be a hostile or two toward the parking lot's south-western corner. Continue until you reach the concrete wall west of the stadium; use it for cover.

Several hostiles lurk behind sandbag barriers on the western side of the large concrete wall. Position your Ghost team along the wall to engage the enemies while you send the other team to take cover behind the concrete barricades to the enemy's south. If necessary, use smoke to provide concealment so you can get your teams into position. Move to take cover behind another concrete barricade in the south.

If you can't shoot the enemies behind the sandbags, frag 'em.

Move a team forward to make sure the area around the sand-bags is clear.

From these positions, you should be able to take out the enemies guarding the last two AA vehicles. Throw frag grenades to kill the enemies hiding behind the sandbags. Once it looks clear, move one of your teams forward to check it out. There may still be a hostile or two near the AA vehicles, so secure the area. Before placing the charges on the vehicles, move your teams to a position along the concrete wall to the east and then blow the two vehicles so the journalist can be extracted.

Plant C4 charges on the two remaining AA vehicles.

# 3. MOVE TO THE RALLY POINT

### MAP SECTION B

## Orders

Move to the rally point to meet up with the Ghost truck.

Resupply at the Ghost truck.

A Blackhawk arrives to take the journalist to safety. Now order your teams to regroup on you; lead them to the eastern side of the parking lot, where a convoy with the Ghost truck is waiting. The Mexican Army commander is taking back his two soldiers, which leave with the convoy. However, you have to wait for extraction. Not only can you resupply, you can also modify your team—which is a good idea considering what you face next. In addition to a rifleman, take along the gunner and the anti-tank gunner. As for you, some heavy firepower would be nice. Try out the M468. It uses a large round for increased lethality. Fill out the rest of your load with a secondary weapon and an offensive pack of grenades.

# 4. HOLD POSITION UNTIL EXTRACTION

### MAP SECTION B

## Orders

A Blackhawk is on the way. Hold your current position until it arrives.

**Shoot the gunners on top of the tanks and order your anti-tank gunner to engage them.**

As the convoy leaves, your team is left behind to make sure the convoy's rear is not attacked. However, you have trouble of your own. Enemies are approaching from the southeast. Order your team to take cover behind the concrete walls. In addition to hostile infantry, two tanks approach your position. If you brought along the anti-tank gunner, order him to attack one. You can shoot at the gunners on top of the tanks—just be sure to stay behind cover.

The Apache takes out the last tank.

If you can hold out for a bit, air support is on the way. When it arrives, an AH-64 Apache will be tasked to you. Select it on the Cross-Com and order it to attack each of the tanks in turn. It leaves once both tanks are destroyed. Finish off any enemy infantry in the area.

# 5. REACH THE EXTRACTION POINT

## MAP SECTION C

### Orders

Move your team to the new extraction point.

Lead your team across the overpass to the western part of the map.

Order your team to move from cover to cover as you advance.

Due to the heavy enemy presence in the area around the stadium, your extraction point has been moved to the church in the south-east. Before heading out, make sure the area is clear of hostiles. You don't want them attacking you from behind while you make your exit.

The rooftop is now clear.

Advance around the back of these buildings rather than advancing down the main street headed south.

To get to the church, you must cross over a highway to the western side of the area. Take the northern overpass and use the concrete barricades for cover as you advance toward the intersection. The enemies are south and west of this area. Move to the corner of the building on your left, peek around to the south, and shoot the hostile on the rooftop, who is waiting to snipe at your team. Continue west across the street with your team to engage hostiles behind the buildings.

Send your team down to this corner to locate and then engage the enemy near the major intersection.

Use the CFV to see what your team can see and give them attack orders.

Stay as far west as possible as your team advances south. The westernmost alleys are blocked, so use the one just west of the street and send your team to the corner of the wall west of the intersection where six roads meet. Your soldiers detect a couple hostiles behind some concrete walls. Order the team to attack while you head east toward the intersection itself to flank the enemy.

The Blackhawk takes fire at the extraction point.

Order your team to try to shoot down the enemy helicopters.

Once these hostiles have been neutralized, it is a straight shot to the church. Order your team to regroup on you and then head south. Follow the street all the way and then move in toward the steps leading up to the church. The Blackhawk waits for you. As you approach, the Blackhawk comes under fire and crash lands somewhere else. However, you have more pressing matters. Enemy helicopters are dropping off infantry to the north of the church.

Get your team behind cover near the church and then engage the enemy infantry.

Shoot as many of the enemies as possible while staying behind cover.

Quickly lead your team up the steps to the church and take cover behind the stone planters. Set your team's ROE to Assault mode and begin killing hostiles as they approach. As enemy helicopters come into view, order your team to attack them. Your anti-tank gunner may be able to shoot them down. However, your main task now is just to survive. As long as you stay behind cover and keep shooting hostiles, you will make it.

A friendly Humvee is on the way to extract you. Listen to the updates from the driver so you know how close he is to your location and when he finally arrives.

# 6. EXTRACT TO THE HUMVEE

### MAP SECTION C

### Orders

Move to the Humvee for extraction.

**Get to the Humvee to complete the mission.**

When the Humvee finally arrives, it parks just north of the church near your location. Take some shots at the hostiles to keep their heads down and then throw a few smoke grenades to the north of the Humvee to provide some concealment. Once the smoke fills the air, stand up and run to the Humvee. You automatically climb aboard, and the driver races you through the enemy-filled streets of Juarez as you try to make your escape to safety.

An enemy Havoc gunship chases after your humvee as you try to get away.

While it looks like you lose the enemy helicopter, it is waiting for you on the outskirts of town.

# On Your Own

## GRAW2 ▶ SINGLE PLAYER
### MISSION 7: ON YOUR OWN

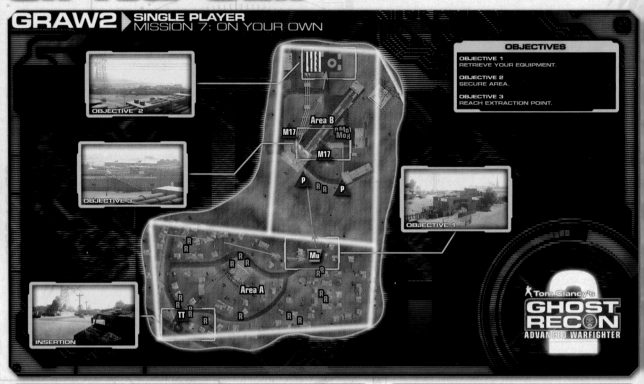

**OBJECTIVES**

**OBJECTIVE 1**
RETRIEVE YOUR EQUIPMENT.

**OBJECTIVE 2**
SECURE AREA.

**OBJECTIVE 3**
REACH EXTRACTION POINT.

OBJECTIVE 2 · OBJECTIVE 3 · OBJECTIVE 1 · INSERTION · Area A · Area B

## LEGEND

- ◉ = Insertion Point
- ◎ = Extraction Point
- **Mu** = MULE
- **R** = Rifleman (Soldats)
- **Mo** = Mortar (Soldats)
- **TT** = Troop Transport (Soldats)
- **P** = Panhard (Soldats)
- **M17** = Mi17 Helicopter (Soldats)

## OBJECTIVES

1. Move to the rally point.
2. Reach the MULE.
3. Reach extraction point.
4. Destroy the choppers.
5. Extract with Blackhawk 9.

## MISSION BRIEFING

You survived the attack and now must fight with only your weapons—not electronic detection devices or your HUD.

The situation is critical. Your Blackhawk for extraction has been shot down, and your HUD has been damaged. You're on your own to reach the extraction point and survive the mysteriously highly trained mercenaries who've joined the rebels.

## 1. MOVE TO THE RALLY POINT

### MAP SECTION A

### Orders

Advance through a settlement on the outskirts of Juarez to reach the rally point.

Take cover behind the Humvee wreckage.

**Without your HUD, you will have to watch for the enemies on your own. Look for movement.**

As your Humvee raced away from the ambush in Juarez, it was attacked by an enemy helicopter and destroyed. Luckily, you, your driver, and the rest of the team survived. Most of your electronic gear, including your helmet headset, was destroyed in the crash. As a result, you must fight without the aid of intel on your HUD and locate targets with your eyes and ears. You still have your primary weapon from the previous mission, which you need right away since a truckload of hostiles is inbound on your position.

**Destroy the truck as soon as it comes into sight.**

**Use the scope to hit enemies at a distance—especially if they are hiding behind cover.**

Take cover behind the wreckage of the Humvee and begin targeting the enemies. The truck stops to the north of your position and starts unloading infantry. Open up on the truck and destroy it—hopefully killing a few hostiles when it blows up. Then pick off the enemies one by one. Since you don't have the benefit of your HUD, you have to watch for the enemies on your own. Use muzzle flashes and movement to find the hostiles, then fire.

**Take time at each position to study the area ahead, looking for enemies that might be waiting for you as well as cover you can use.**

**Move from cover to cover, killing all of the hostiles you encounter along the way.**

Your driver helps by calling out enemies as he locates them, so listen to his cues. He also lets you know when the area is clear so you can advance toward the rally point. Since you do not need to clear out this entire settlement to complete your first objective, focus on just getting to the rally point. The best route is to move north along the area's western edge. Head toward the first house and quickly take cover along one of its walls, watching for hostiles to the north and east. If it is clear, stand and move quickly to the next bit of cover. Continue advancing to the northern edge of the area, then head east. Running from cover to cover makes it more difficult for the enemy to hit you. Pausing and watching at each place of cover helps you scout out enemies, lets you plan which cover you want to move to next, and gives your driver a chance to catch up to you.

## TIP

Don't leave your driver behind during this mission. Although you can't give him orders, he will follow you and engage enemies on his own. He will also warn you of enemies you may not be able to see.

Watch out for enemies right next to the building where your rally point is located.

The hostiles usually move about in groups of two or three. So if you see and kill one, wait and look for others before moving. The rally point is in a larger structure with walls made of corrugated metal. Head up the ramp and enter to complete your first objective.

# 2. REACH THE MULE

### MAP SECTION A

### Orders

Load up on equipment and supplies carried by the MULE.

Pick up a rocket launcher from the MULE.

Inside the rally point building you find a MULE that has been sent there for you to use. Open the back and grab yourself some new weapons. For the next phase of this mission, take along a Zeus T2 rocket launcher, an MP5A3 submachine gun for a secondary weapon, and an offensive pack of grenades. The MULE is now tasked to you, and you have regained some functionality with your Cross-Com. It can be used to give orders to the MULE.

# 3. REACH EXTRACTION POINT

### MAP SECTION B

### Orders

Advance north to the new extraction point.

**Armored cars block your way to the extraction point.**

A new extraction point has been set at the industrial installation north of your position. You must clear out some enemies along the way—including a couple of armored cars. Move north and take cover behind the wrecked vehicle. A Panhard to the northeast starts moving toward your position, firing its machine gun. Take aim with the Zeus and fire. Keep the vehicle centered in your sights to guide the missile to its target. One hit will take it out. Reload another rocket and fire at the second vehicle due north.

Maintain your aim as you fire and until the rocket hits the target and explodes.

A couple of hostile infantry are also to the north. Take them out with your submachine gun. Fire it in quick bursts for greater accuracy. It will take a few tries to hit them. You can also advance north and engage them at a closer range, but be careful since they can fire at you while you are out in the open. Furthermore, enemies to the north are now firing mortar rounds at you—so keep moving to avoid being hit.

Advance with your submachine gun to eliminate the hostiles as you try to avoid being hit by mortar fire.

## TIP

As you take cover behind the wrecked vehicle, order the MULE to regroup on you. After you destroy the two armored cars, switch to an assault rifle or sniper rifle and use it to kill the two infantry to the north.

Move into this underground area for protection from the mortars.

Bring the MULE to your location.

As you move north toward the extraction point, you need to find cover from the mortar fire. Locate the road leading northwest once you get to the installation and follow it into an area under one of the structures. This provides some additional protection. Order the MULE to join you there. Use it to heal yourself if necessary. Continue through the underground area to the second opening. As you are about to exit, you receive a new objective.

# 4. DESTROY THE CHOPPERS

MAP SECTION B

### Orders

Shoot down the two enemy helicopters to clear the area for your extraction.

The shadows cast by the choppers show when they have passed—letting you know it's safe to move out and attack.

**When a helicopter starts firing, move under cover or you will get hit and possibly killed.**

Two enemy helicopters have arrived on the scene. Until they have been neutralized, you can't extract. Get a full load of rockets from the MULE and move out through the opening where you first entered this underground area. There are two Mi-17 helicopter gunships looking for you. Stay near the entrance so you can duck back in for protection. Listen for the choppers to approach and even watch for their shadows outside the underground area.

**One hit usually does the job.**

**Shoot down the second chopper as well to clear the way for your extraction.**

The helicopters circle around looking for you. As soon as you locate one, take aim with your Zeus and fire. Keep the chopper in your sights until the rocket hits. Shooting down a helicopter with this anti-tank weapon can be difficult. If you miss, duck back under cover while you reload and then set up for another shot. It should take just one good hit to bring a helicopter down. It may not explode immediately, but instead move away and crash. However, if you are uncertain if you got a good hit, fire another rocket to

make sure. Use the same tactic for both helicopters. If you take hits or need more rockets, heal and resupply at the MULE.

# 5. EXTRACT WITH BLACKHAWK 9

MAP SECTION B

## Orders

Advance to the extraction point to board a Blackhawk.

**Follow the pipeline to the extraction zone.**

Now that both helicopters have been shot down, the area is clear for your Blackhawk to touch down. Exit the underground area through the northeast opening and follow the large pipes to the northeast where Blackhawk 9 is waiting to pick you up on top of a small hill.

**This Blackhawk will fly you out of the area.**

## NOTE

Before you move to the extraction point, be sure to have a submachine gun or an assault rifle as your active weapon. There are four hostiles at a mortar position east of the underground structure. If you stay away from them, they won't bother you, but be prepared in case they spot you and attack.

# Failure Is *Not* an Option

## OBJECTIVES

1. Secure area.
2. Protect convoy.
3. Shoot choppers.

## MISSION BRIEFING

**Fly back into Juarez to bring back what was left behind.**

You've managed to put yourself in safety, but you're sent back on the battlefield to check the crash site where the Blackhawk has been shot down and recover the crew as soon as possible. No one shall be left behind.

## 1. SECURE AREA

### Orders

Secure the area by neutralizing all enemies in this part of Juarez.

**Take out the anti-tank gunner on this roof first.**

This is another mission where you ride in a Blackhawk and man the chain gun. However, this mission is more dangerous and challenging than the previous aerial mission. The first phase has you flying over the city of Juarez and engaging primarily infantry as well as some trucks carrying these hostiles. Remember that the chain gun takes a couple seconds to spin up and start shooting, so pull the trigger early and fire in long bursts, pausing only when there are no enemies or when the gun needs to cool down.

**Clear the street.**

As you approach the water tower, be ready for action. An anti-tank gunner fires rockets at your helicopter from the rooftop near the water tower. Take out him and the other soldiers that appear near him. Next clear the street below. You face just infantry to begin with, but a truck approaches from the left. Shoot it to destroy the vehicle and kill the infantry inside before they can disembark.

### TIP

Aim for the parked cars along the streets where there are hostiles nearby. The cars explode, killing several enemies in a single blast.

Another truck arrives—take it out.

When you approach an area with a fountain below, the Blackhawk hovers over it. Watch for hostiles to appear on the roof and down on the streets. Another truck arrives, so blow it up as well. Finish up all the remaining infantry and then wait for the Blackhawk to continue to the next area.

Watch for hostiles to appear on the rooftops.

# 2. PROTECT CONVOY

## Orders

Fly escort to a convoy of U.S. Strykers and protect them from hostile infantry and vehicles.

Take out the Mowag ahead of the convoy and then mop up the infantry as you circle back around.

Intelligence informs you that the Blackhawk and crew have been taken away by the enemy. It is time to head back to the United States. Your new objective is to make sure the convoy of three Strykers sent to retrieve the Blackhawk makes it back as well. You approach them from behind. Be ready to shoot at the enemies blocking the road ahead—a Mowag armored personnel carrier along with infantry. Shoot at and destroy the Mowag; this takes out most of the infantry as well. The Blackhawk then circles the area, allowing you to mop up the enemy infantry on the streets and some on the rooftops.

The Panhards drive right alongside your Strykers, making it tougher for you to hit them.

As the convoy continues, be ready for more enemies. Several Panhards appear one at a time and approach the convoy. Try to hit them before they get close to the convoy. Once they are driving alongside your Strykers, be careful with your fire so you don't hit your own men. The last Panhard drives on the grass to the side of the convoy. Once it is destroyed, let the chain gun cool down for a bit.

A couple more Mowags come in behind the convoy.

Take out these infantry as the Blackhawk comes in low.

As the convoy makes a left turn near some warehouses, get ready for a couple of Mowag APCs to appear. Both come in from behind the convoy after it completes the turn—one from the left and the other from the right. Destroy the left APC first, and then the right. Finally, mow down the infantry that emerge from the warehouse as your Blackhawk descends to give you a good shot.

The last Mowag and infantry are near a gas station. Destroy the Mowag to set off a much larger explosion, killing all of the infantry.

As the Blackhawk pulls away, get ready to engage another group of hostiles. This time, destroy the Mowag and the resulting explosion will take out all the infantry. The convoy is now safe from ground targets and is getting close to the border. Let your guns cool down for the next threat.

# 3. Shoot Choppers

## Orders

Shoot down the two enemy helicopters and protect the convoy.

This first chopper goes after your convoy. Shoot it down quickly.

The last two enemies you face are also your toughest—two Mi-17 gunships. The first helicopter flies down and attacks the Strykers directly. As soon as you can get it in your sights, start attacking. The helicopters have a lot more firepower than the previous enemies, and if you don't shoot down the first chopper quickly, it will destroy one of your Strykers and the mission will end in failure. Keep up a constant stream of fire and the chopper will go down before your gun overheats.

Try to get as many hits on the second helicopter while it is in range. The more you get now, the easier it is to destroy later.

The chase along the highway is where you must outshoot the enemy helicopter, sending it into the ground before it shoots your Blackhawk down.

The second gunship stays at a distance for a while. It is trying to get you to overheat your guns while firing at long range. Shoot when it first comes into sight and is close to try to cause as much damage as possible. However, keep those guns cool as it pulls away. As you near the highway, get ready. The helicopter flies sideways toward you, firing away. This is the toughest part of the mission. You must keep your fire on the enemy at all times to cause maximum damage before it can shoot down your Blackhawk. If you kept the gun cool until this part, you won't have to worry about it overheating. Just keep shooting until the copter goes down. Your Blackhawk and the convoy can now safely cross the border back into the United States and plan your next mission.

The convoy arrives safely to cross the border.

THE CAMPAIGN

# Get Me Rosen

## GRAW2 ▶ SINGLE PLAYER
### MISSION 9: GET ME ROSEN

### OBJECTIVES

**OBJECTIVE 1**
REACH DOWNED HELICOPTER AND PLACE A DEMO CHARGE TO DESTROY THE WRECKAGE.

**OBJECTIVE 2**
ELIMINATE ENEMIES PATROLLING THE HACIENDA PROPERTY.

**OBJECTIVE 3**
MEET UP WITH THE GHOSTS TO SECURE ROSEN.

**OBJECTIVE 4**
REACH ROSEN'S POSITION AND SECURE HIM.

**OBJECTIVE 5**
SECURE THE HACIENDA.

**OBJECTIVE 6**
REACH EXTRACTION ZONE.

## LEGEND

- ◉ = Insertion Point
- ◎ = Extraction Point
- **Gt** = Ghost Truck
- **R** = Rifleman (Soldats)
- **G** = Machine Gunner (Soldats)
- **Gc** = Guncam Man (Mercenaries)
- **Mk** = Marksman (Soldats)
- **TT** = Transport Truck

## OBJECTIVES

1. Destroy Blackhawk 5's remnants.
2. Take out enemy sentries.
3. Link up with team.
4. Find Rosen.
5. Secure area for extraction.
6. Extract Rosen.

## MISSION BRIEFING

SAMALAYUCA DESIERTO
CHIHUAHUA STATE

This mission takes you out of the city and back into the desert.

The Blackhawk wreckage has been removed by the rebels, who plan to show on TV the actual helicopter and Rosen, the last crewman, to prove that Americans are responsible for the violence in Juarez. Your mission is to destroy remnants of the chopper and get Rosen back.

## 1. DESTROY BLACKHAWK 5'S REMNANTS

### MAP SECTION A

### Orders

Locate and destroy the remnants of Blackhawk 5 to prevent the rebels from using it to blame America for the violence in Juarez.

The first part of this mission is solo. You must move in on the building containing the wreckage of Blackhawk 5 and destroy it. Several hostiles guard it, so you must neutralize all of them before completing this objective. You want to engage enemies at long range as much as possible, so take along a counter-sniper rifle such as the SR A550. You also need some close-range firepower, preferably silenced, so choose the MP5A3 SD for your secondary weapon. Finally, select the offensive grenade pack.

**Head north to locate the first hostiles patrolling the eastern area.**

You have been given command of a UAV. Use it to scout out the enemies and then monitor their movements while you operate in the area. Start off by sending the UAV north and scanning in CFV. A couple of hostiles patrol the area north of you and east of the target building. Eliminate them first. Once the UAV is detected, switch out of CFV and leave it there to keep track of the two hostiles. There is not a lot of cover between you and the enemies other than the lay of the land. Advance north, watching the two red intel markers on your HUD. As you get near the enemies, drop prone and crawl forward until you can see their heads. Take aim and shoot. You may have to move forward a bit to get the second one—just stay low.

**Your counter-sniper rifle can take out enemies behind cover.**

Have the UAV scan around the building; leave it hovering over the area. From your position to the building's northeast, see if you can clear out any more hostiles, then withdraw. Head south and use the metal wall to the building's east as cover as you clear out more hostiles. Move south, stopping at each edge of the wall to see if you can take out more hostiles. Remember that your sniper rifle can penetrate walls and crates, so shoot right through them.

**Take out these hostiles patrolling north of the building.**

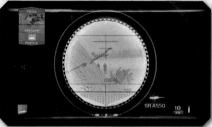

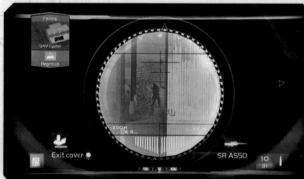

**Make your way around to the south of the building, using cover as you go.**

Now that this part of the map is clear, get up and continue to the map's northern edge, then cautiously advance west. Use the UAV to scout the area around the building and the hills to the west of it. There are several hostiles around the building and an enemy marksman on the hill. Once again drop prone and crawl west, engaging a few hostiles north of the building. However, keep track of the marksman on the hill. He is a threat to you. As soon as you can get a shot, take it or he will shoot you.

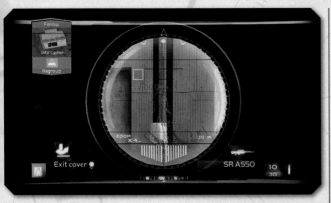

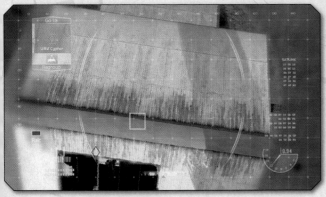

**If you can detect hostiles inside the building, shoot right through the thin walls to kill them.**

By this time, you should have eliminated all of the enemies to the north, east, and south of the building. The rest are either to the west or inside. Approach from the southeast, taking cover behind crates as you move. Use the UAV to scan over the building to see if you can locate more hostiles inside. Finish off any hostiles on the outside and then move around to the door on the building's western side. Switch to your submachine gun now. The interior is dark, so use your ENVG to light it up. The western door leads into a smaller room. Make sure it is clear, enter, and move to the next door, which leads into the larger area where the Blackhawk is.

## TIP

Use your ears and be patient while clearing out the building. It may seem empty, but if you can hear voices, there is still someone around. There is no need to rush, even though your commanding officer may ask you what the holdup is. Take your time.

**The interior of the building is dark, so use your ENVG.**

Usually at least one or two hostiles still lurk inside. Frequently scan with the UAV to see if you can see them or if they are leaving the building. Using the doorway as cover, shoot any hostiles near the helicopter. Those that survive may exit the building and try to come around through another doorway. Again scan with the UAV; eliminate hostiles by moving through or around the building until you can bring them into your sights. Once the area is clear, place a C4 charge on the Blackhawk and get out of the building before it detonates.

**Place a charge on the Blackhawk.**

# 2. TAKE OUT ENEMY SENTRIES

### MAP SECTION B

### Orders

Eliminate the sentries at the two enemy outposts in the northwest and southeast.

**Approach the northwestern outpost through this gap.**

The next part of the mission is to clear two outposts in the area so you can receive reinforcements. Start off with the one in the northwest since it offers a bit more cover as you approach it. Select your sniper rifle and move out. Scan the area between you and the outpost with the UAV and leave it hovering over the enemy position to monitor it.

# NOTE

A truck of reinforcements arrives at whichever outpost you approach first. Engaging these hostiles in the northwest makes the southeast much easier.

Take cover behind this wooden wall while you snipe at the enemies around the outpost.

Move around to the south and use the submachine gun for engaging at close range.

There is a gap in the ridgeline to the east of the outpost. Take cover behind the wooden wall and take out nearby hostiles patrolling this area as you peek around the side. Eliminate as many as you can from this position, then advance, taking cover behind a wall to the south of the building around which the hostiles are positioned. Watch for a couple of hostiles that may approach from the south. Keep scanning with the UAV to see if these new arrivals are trying to sneak up on you. Continue to move around, using cover as you clear out as many hostiles as possible with your sniper rifle. Then move in on the building and use your submachine gun to take out any remaining threats to secure this area.

# TIP

Destroy the truck with frag grenades. The explosion will kill any hostiles hiding behind it. Don't use your sniper rifle—it would take up too much ammo, which you need for the next outpost.

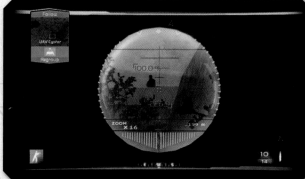

Shoot at hostiles to the southeast from as far away as possible.

THE CAMPAIGN

These cars provide cover as you engage the hostiles around the southeastern outpost. There are more, closer to the buildings, which you can use as well.

Move in and finish off any survivors with your submachine gun.

Take control of the UAV and fly it along the road to the southeast. A couple of hostiles patrol the road; however, once the firefight in the northwest starts, they usually move in from the south. If that didn't happen, keep the UAV over them and advance to kill them with your sniper rifle. Take the UAV over the outpost to locate four hostiles. Once you have found all of them, release the UAV to hover at high altitude over the area while you approach from the northwest. You can possibly kill some of the rebels from the intersection just southeast of the first outpost. The more you can take out at long range, the easier it will be when you get closer. A couple of abandoned cars along the road provide cover for you. From behind these wrecks, snipe at as many hostiles as possible. Then move in and take out the rest with your submachine gun.

# 3. LINK UP WITH TEAM

## Orders

Move to the rally point and link up with the Ghost Squad.

Meet up with the Ghost truck to choose your team.

Now that the roads into the area are clear, a convoy moves toward the center of the map. Move to its location at the rally point and approach the Ghost truck to prepare for the next part of the mission. In addition to a rifleman, take along a grenadier. For the third slot, go with either the marksman or another rifleman. Pick an assault rifle of your choice and take along a silenced submachine gun as well.

## NOTE

Whatever weapons and team you select here carry over to the next mission—so keep your options open and don't choose anything too specialized.

# 4. FIND ROSEN

## MAP SECTION C

### Orders

Locate Rosen in the hacienda and prepare for extraction.

Approach the hacienda from the east.

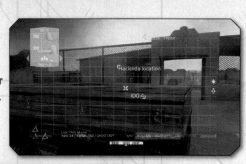

Use CFV to see what your team can see.

The low wall provides some cover for you as you approach the building.

Take out the hostiles around this first building.

Rosen is being held in the hacienda complex in the map's southwestern quadrant. While the main approach is from the north, there is also a gap in the ridgeline to the east of the complex. Order your team to regroup on you and then lead it to this gap. Scan the area around the building near the gap with the UAV to locate all of the hostiles. Once you have detected them, move your team in. Look for a container to the east of the building where your teammates can take cover. Keep them in Recon mode and use the CFV to see what they can see. Move to the building's entrance and switch to Assault mode so they will open fire. Peek around the corner of the opening and help take out enemies. Move your team in to take cover inside the building, and work together to flank the remaining enemies—they are behind cover and difficult to neutralize.

Clear out hostiles as you approach the pool area.

Come at the hacienda from the east, taking out the hostiles on the rooftop.

Once the area around this building is secure, head south toward the swimming pool area. Scan it and the area to the west for hostiles. There are usually only a couple of enemies. Take them out and then focus on the main building. Hostiles patrol the rooftop and the grounds to the north. Position your team behind cover and then move in as the Ghosts open fire. Make your way to the stairs leading up to the roof. One stairway is along the eastern side in the southeastern corner. Once on the roof, order your team to regroup on you; use the low walls as cover to clear the remainder of the roof.

THE CAMPAIGN

The rooftop is clear, so look down into the interior of the hacienda for more enemies.

Position your team along the northern walls on the rooftop and engage enemies to the north of the hacienda.

Continue to scan the area with the UAV to make sure you got all of the hostiles around the hacienda. Once it's clear, position your team along the rooftop's northern wall in Recon mode. Scan to the north with the UAV to locate any additional hostiles and engage as many as you can. Call out targets to your team to attack.

Rosen is inside the hacienda. Move to him and then head back up to the roof.

Rosen moves to hide behind this structure on the southern part of the roof. He is safe, so you don't have to worry about him.

Now get Rosen. He is inside the hacienda. Switch to your submachine gun and move down the southeastern stairs to enter through the nearby doorway. Check around corners as you enter and use your ENVG as necessary since the interior is dark. It should be clear, but be ready for an enemy inside that may have avoided detection by the UAV. Move over to Rosen to complete this objective.

# 5. SECURE AREA FOR EXTRACTION

## MAP SECTION C

### Orders

Repel enemy reinforcements and secure the area in order to extract Rosen and the Ghosts.

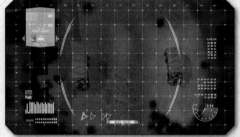

Use the UAV to scan the new arrivals.

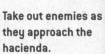

Take out enemies as they approach the hacienda.

Destroying trucks creates explosions that kill nearby hostiles. Order your team, with the grenadier, to attack them.

Once you have found Rosen, he heads to the rooftop and takes cover until the Blackhawk arrives. However, more enemies are inbound. A few trucks approach from the north and start unloading infantry. Get back up to the roof and get ready for a firefight. The hostiles come at you from the north and northeast. Place your team in Assault mode so it fires to the north while you move to cover the northeast. In addition to shooting, throw frag grenades down on the enemy. As your teammates clear the area to the north, move them to the northeast corner and assign them targets to attack. Keep an eye on them—the enemy puts a lot of firepower on the roof, and members of your team may be wounded. Heal them quickly; the low wall provides cover as you give them medical care.

# 6. EXTRACT ROSEN

MAP SECTION C

## Orders

Meet with Rosen at the extraction point.

The Blackhawk is your ticket out of here.

Once you have eliminated the enemies around the hacienda area, the Blackhawk flies in for extraction. Move to the Blackhawk as it lands. Rosen automatically moves to the location as well. Once you get to the helicopter, you have completed the last objective and saved Rosen.

On to the next mission.

# Who the Hell Are These Guys?

## GRAW2 ▶ SINGLE PLAYER
### MISSION 10: WHO THE HELL ARE THESE GUYS?

**OBJECTIVES**

OBJECTIVE 1
DESTROY 2 ADATS OUTPOSTS.

OBJECTIVE 2
REACH VIP'S POSITION.

OBJECTIVE 3
HOLD CURRENT POSITION.

OBJECTIVE 4
REACH SUPPLY POINT: GHOST TRUCK.

OBJECTIVE 5
REACH POSITION.

OBJECTIVE 6
REACH BLACKHAWK FOR EXTRACTION.

Tom Clancy's
GHOST RECON
ADVANCED WARFIGHTER 2

## LEGEND

- ◯ = Insertion Point
- ◉ = Extraction Point
- R = Rifleman (Soldats)
- G = Machine Gunner (Soldats)
- Gf = Machine Gun Fixed (Soldats)
- Gc = Guncam Man (Mercenaries)
- Ad = Adats (Soldats)
- M = Mowag (Soldats)

## OBJECTIVES

1. Take out anti-air threats.
2. Take position at the rebel HQ.
3. Hold the area.
4. Move to rally point.
5. Reach rebel leader's position.
6. Enter Blackhawk 9.
7. Secure the area.
8. Shoot down the rebel leader.

## MISSION BRIEFING

CIUDAD JUAREZ
CENTRO HISTORICO                    04:06:08

You are flying back into Juarez.

Thanks to the Mexican journalist you extracted, we've got solid intel on where the rebel leaders are hiding the nukes. You're being sent into Juarez as part of a large-scale joint operation to neutralize all the nuclear devices.

## 1. TAKE OUT ANTI-AIR THREATS

**MAP SECTION A**

### Orders

Destroy four AA vehicles to clear the way for other troops.

You have a Stryker tasked to you in addition to your Ghost team.

This is one of the biggest missions. You start off with the same team and weapons that you had at the end of the previous mission. In addition, you have a Stryker. While it has a lot of firepower that will help you advance through the city, it is also vulnerable to anti-tank weaponry—so make sure an area is free from these units before moving the Stryker forward.

You can look down on the enemy from this elevated walkway.

Order your team to regroup on you and order the Stryker to move ahead. It will go for a bit and then stop. Meanwhile, lead your team east down the road and then up a stairway along the road's left side. At the top, turn around and move west a bit to take position along the wall on the right. To the north below you is the first concentration of enemy troops. Send your team behind cover along the wall so it can locate all of the enemies.

## TIP

There are no anti-tank gunners in this first concentration of hostiles, so it is safe to move your Stryker in to help attack.

The view from the Stryker lets you see what it can see and allows you to order it to fire at targets.

Add your firepower to the attack on the enemy below.

Order the Stryker to move ahead again, and use the CFV to check out what it can see. As soon as you see enemies from the Stryker's CFV, order it to fire on them. Then switch your Ghosts' ROE to Assault and they will attack as well. Add your own firepower. A gunner sits on top of a structure opposite you; take him out early in the fight since he can cause the most damage to your team. Keep fighting until all hostiles have been eliminated.

**Move your team down from the walkway and around the corner to clear out the hostiles.**

Order your team back into Recon mode and have it follow you down the stairs to the west to street level. Continue along the road to where it makes a turn to the northeast. Position your teammates behind planters so they can locate several hostiles up ahead. Bring the Stryker forward to help take them out. As before, order your team to Assault and use your weapon to finish off the resistance in this area.

Anti-tank gunners await up ahead near the AA vehicles.

Take out the sentry on the walkway to clear a way for your team.

Eliminate all of the enemies below.

The next area contains some anti-tank gunners, so keep the Stryker back for now. With your team in Recon mode, lead it up the stairs along the road where you just took out the enemy riflemen and then to a wall to the northwest. A single hostile patrols the walkway ahead of you. Take him out and then order your team-mates to take positions behind planters so they can fire on the enemy below to the north. The anti-tank gunners are your main targets. There are two of them, so try to take them out first. Leave the Stryker behind just in case you did not get all of the anti-tank gunners. You and your team can clear the area. Watch for enemies to try to flank you down at the end of the walkway. Move around as needed to get the right angle to clear out the enemy below. When it looks clear, order your team to move to the sandbags near the AA vehicles while you cover your squad from the elevated walkway.

Two down—two more to go.

Now that the area is clear, order the Stryker to move forward as you head down the stairs to the northwest and continue to the AA vehicles. Order your team to move to a safe distance while you place a C4 charge on the left-hand AA vehicle. When this vehicle explodes, it destroys the second one.

Move the team east toward the next objective.

Use the Stryker to take out these two hostiles on your flank.

The remaining two AA vehicles are to the east. Lead your team toward them. Before you go too far, send your Stryker ahead to check things out. Use the CFV to monitor the Stryker's progress. As it turns south, look for a couple of hostiles ahead and order the Stryker to take them out. This clears the way for your team to move into position without being hit in the flank. Move through some rubble and position your teammates behind a wall across the street from the objective. Put them in Assault mode and then bring the Stryker forward to help clear out the area. Take position behind cover and fire at your own targets while also assigning targets for your team and the Stryker.

This last hostile can be tough to kill.

**Blow up these last two AA vehicles.**

After you clear out this area, there may be one hostile up on a walkway above the objective. He can be tough to eliminate if he is hiding. Order your team to target him and then move forward until you are almost under him; throw a frag grenade so it hits the wall above the enemy and drops right back down onto him to explode. After throwing it, move back in case the grenade lands at street level rather than on the upper walkway. Send your team north to take a position along a wall to the right of the road while you blow up the AA vehicles with C4. The vehicles are far enough apart this time that you will have to set a charge on each. Just be sure you are away before the charges go off.

## TIP

Don't hide behind the truck after planting charges. It explodes when the AA vehicles are destroyed.

# 2. TAKE POSITION AT THE REBEL HQ

MAP SECTION B

### Orders

Move your team to the rebel HQ.

**U.S. helicopters are attacking the rebel HQ and looking for the nukes.**

Now that you have completed the objective of destroying the rebels' anti-aircraft capability, U.S. air units can move in on the rebel headquarters. Your next job is to lead your team to the headquarters, meet up with the other troops, and help where needed. Advance north along the road until you can see the objective below, then turn west to find stairs down to the lower level. A U.S. Littlebird helicopter is attacking the area, making sure it is clear. Continue to the objective location and wait for further orders. As you progress, your Stryker is recalled for operations elsewhere.

**Advance to this position.**

# 3. HOLD THE AREA

MAP SECTION B

### Orders

Hold this position until Bravo Team secures the nukes.

**Take cover behind the concrete barricades.**

Bravo Team is inside the building getting the nukes ready for transport out of here. However, the enemy is moving in troops to stop you. Your job is to eliminate the waves of attacking hostiles so that Bravo Team can do its job.

Fire on the enemies as they approach. You have plenty of targets.

The attacks come from the west, so position your team and yourself behind concrete barricades for cover and get ready to fight. Set the ROE to Assault so everyone can open fire as soon as they see targets. Stay behind cover and fire at the enemies as they come. Give targets for your team as necessary. There is no need to move around since the enemy keeps coming toward you. Keep fighting until all hostiles have been neutralized.

## TIP

Order your team to attack the trucks. When the vehicles explode, they may kill nearby enemies.

# 4. MOVE TO RALLY POINT

MAP SECTION B

## Orders

Advance to the rally point.

Head around to the rally point.

Bravo Team has successfully secured one of the nuclear devices and is on its way to the second one. You have been ordered to move to the rally point and meet up with the Ghost truck for some resupply. Lead your team to the rally point and approach the truck. You now get to select your team. The next phase is pretty tough, so in addition to your rifleman, take along your gunner and the combat medic. As for yourself, try out the MK14 EBR. It has a powerful round that is good for taking down enemies. The rest of your equipment is up to you. You have a couple of support units tasked to you. The first is an M1A2 Abrams main battle tank, and the other is a Littlebird attack helicopter.

# 5. REACH REBEL LEADER'S POSITION

MAP SECTION C

## Orders

Advance on the rebel leader's position.

## Secondary Objective

Neutralize fleeing vehicles.

You have been given a tank to command. Use it to lead the way.

While Bravo Team was able to secure one of the nukes and kill a rebel leader, the other rebel leader has escaped through the sewers to a location near the airport. You must use your units to fight through the enemy, clearing a path to where the nuke is headed. Along the way you face some Mowag APCs and lots of infantry. However, with your heavy firepower from the tank and attack helicopter, you should have no trouble.

## TIP

Use the tank as cover for yourself and your team.

**Order your support units to take out the enemy armor.**

Move the tank forward and use the CFV to monitor it. Assign targets from this view. As you advance into the area containing the enemy, the smoke makes it hazy and difficult to see. Keep yourself and your team behind cover. As soon as the first Mowag comes into view, target it for the tank and the M1A2 will move forward to destroy it.

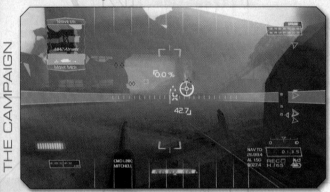

**The CFV of the tank gives you a good view of the battle and lets you assign targets for the tank—either infantry or vehicles.**

Use the Littlebird to locate enemies ahead, giving it movement orders from the tactical map. Not only can it engage infantry, but it also has the firepower to destroy enemy vehicles, including the Mowags that move into the area to drop off more infantry.

**Take out enemy infantry as you advance with your team.**

**The objective location is on the far side of the hangar building.**

Continue advancing toward the objective location. Move your team and yourself up, along with the tank. There are no anti-tank gunners in this area, so let the tank lead the way with the Littlebird scouting out targets and engaging them. Usually some hostiles hide out in the large hangar building. Use the Littlebird to take out enemies outside while you and your team clear out the inside. The tank advances right through the building to the other side.

# 6. ENTER BLACKHAWK 9

## Orders

Continue advancing toward the airport, where Blackhawk 9 will pick you up.

As you reach the objective location, you receive word that the Mexican Army troops who were following the rebel leader through the sewers have been cut off. You must now get to the airport, where Blackhawk 9 is waiting to take you aboard for further operations.

**Move your team forward to take out the anti-tank gunners.**

THE CAMPAIGN

Use the Littlebird to attack the Mowag.

To get to the airport, your troops must advance down a narrow roadway leading southwest. Send the Littlebird ahead to locate a Mowag and a couple of anti-tank gunners. Keep your tank back until you take out those gunners. Move your team forward, eliminating hostiles as you advance. Order the Littlebird to take out the Mowag as you approach, and begin firing on the anti-tank gunners. Once they are eliminated, you can send the tank the rest of the way.

The Littlebird can also be ordered to attack the trucks and infantry near the objective location.

A few trucks arrive near the objective location and start unloading troops. Order the Littlebird to take out the trucks while you move forward with the tank. Again, use the CFV to give targeting orders. Finally, move in with your team and mop up any remaining hostiles at the southern end of this area. Once it is clear, leave your troops behind and head up the stairs leading to the landing zone, where Blackhawk 9 will pick you up.

Head up these stairs to the LZ.

# 7. Secure the Area

## Orders

Secure the area while Bravo Team searches for the last nuke.

You ride in the Blackhawk for the rest of the mission.

Since the Mexican Army troops were unable to follow the nuke all the way because the rebels collapsed part of the sewer, Bravo Team is moving in to finish the job. However, Bravo needs some air support and you are it. While aboard Blackhawk 9, you man the M134 mini-gun.

Clear out this area, shooting at the buses so they explode.

You fly over the airport loading and unloading zone. Hostiles emerge and fire at you. Take them out with the mini-gun. Target the buses, which will explode and kill nearby hostiles. Keep the gun firing and mop them all up.

**Call in air support on the enemy tanks. There are two you have to take out.**

As you finish up, a tank arrives on the scene. You must take it out before it can harm Bravo Team. Luckily, an F-15 has been tasked to you for air support. Aim at the tank and order the F-15 to attack. More infantry appear, so engage them—but keep an eye out for a second tank. As soon as you see it, call in an air strike on it as well.

**Get the anti-tank gunner before he gets you.**

**More infantry emerge from the second building.**

Hostiles keep appearing—this time near the building. Take them out, but watch your mini-gun heat meter. You don't want to let it get too hot because when infantry begin to appear on the building's roof, one is an anti-tank gunner. Target him first before he can fire or your Blackhawk will be shot down. More hostiles appear around and on a second building. Keep firing at them but watch your heat level again. Another threat is yet to come.

# 8. SHOOT DOWN THE REBEL LEADER

## Orders

Shoot down the Havoc helicopter in which the rebel leader is escaping.

**The chase is on.**

**Keep firing whenever you can put the enemy chopper in your sights.**

While you are gunning at the hostiles near the second building, you see an enemy Havoc attack helicopter take off and leave the airport. Start shooting at it as soon as it is in your sights. When it moves outside your field of fire, let the mini-gun cool down. Try to cause as much damage as possible to it during the chase. Eventually it stops trying to flee and goes on the attack. It hovers and aims itself straight at you. Keep the trigger depressed and rip into the enemy chopper to shoot it down before your Blackhawk goes down instead. This is a tough duel, but you can take down the rebel leader if you manage your gun's heat and keep it on target.

## TIP

When the Havoc is hovering, hold down the aim mode trigger while firing at it to improve your accuracy.

Keep up the fire and send the rebel leader down in flames. Unfortunately, although you killed the leader, the nukes were not aboard the chopper. The search continues.

The Havoc is gunning for you now.

# Codenamed Farallon

## GRAW2 ▶ SINGLE PLAYER
### MISSION 11: CODENAMED FARALLON

**OBJECTIVES**

**OBJECTIVE 1**
ENTER THE COMPLEX AND TAKE OUT ANY SNIPERS OR GUARDS IN THE WAY.

**OBJECTIVE 2**
SECURE FACILITIES. LOCATE, REACH, AND ELIMINATE ENEMIES NEAR DAM.

**OBJECTIVE 3**
USE EMP TO DISABLE COMPUTER.

**OBJECTIVE 4**
DESTROY TWO ENEMY HELICOPTERS.

**OBJECTIVE 5**
REACH A HUMVEE FOR EXTRACTION.

## LEGEND

- ◉ = Insertion Point
- ◎ = Extraction Point
- ℝ = Rifleman (Soldats)
- 𝔾 = Machine Gunner (Soldats)
- 𝕄𝕜 = Marksman (Soldats)
- 𝔾𝕔 = Guncam Man (Mercenaries)

## OBJECTIVES

1. Enter the water purification complex.
2. Secure the water facility.
3. Disable jammer device.
4. Destroy enemy helicopters.
5. Reach extraction point.

## MISSION BRIEFING

This is an urban operation in Texas. To help, you have an additional team under your command.

You've neutralized the rebel *comandante*, but the mercenaries managed to escape with one nuke. Intel says they're planning to transport the nuke to Caballo Butte dam, on U.S. soil in Texas. Your mission is to secure the dam.

## 1. ENTER THE WATER PURIFICATION COMPLEX

**MAP SECTION A**

### Orders

Move into the water purification complex to secure the nuclear device.

Lead your teams south toward the complex.

Take control of the UAV and look for hostiles in the area ahead of you.

This mission takes place on American soil, and you operate in an urban environment. Start off by selecting your team. Take along your standard rifleman, the grenadier, and the combat medic since the fighting will be heavy. Carry an assault rifle with a lot of ammo, a submachine gun or the M1014 shotgun, and an offensive pack of grenades. In addition to your Ghost team, you have been assigned a team of U.S. soldiers and the UAV. This gives you a lot of firepower and flexibility.

Position your teams at these two locations.

Start off by using the UAV to scan the area south of your starting position. Several enemy riflemen roam the courtyard, and a marksman perches on one of the rooftops. Be sure to detect the marksman and most of the other hostiles. With two teams, you can position them in different places so they can work together to hit the enemy from various sides. Advance south from the insertion area and have your teams follow you. Place your Ghost team at the corner of the building near the white pickup truck and the other team at the corner near the jewelry store, then continue west to a walkway through a building, which puts you just north of the marksman.

Start the attack by taking out the marksman.

Help clear out the enemies in the courtyard.

Use the CFV to move your teams forward to cover so they have better shots on the hostiles.

When you are ready, peek around the corner and take out the marksman with a quick shot. Then switch the ROE of both teams to Assault so they start attacking. Take cover along a wall to your left and begin taking out the hostiles in the courtyard area to the east. As necessary, use the CFV to check on your teams and to give them movement orders so they can advance to cover and continue to engage the enemy. Keep this up until all enemies in this section of the map have been eliminated.

If you brought along the combat medic, be sure to patch up your wounded after each engagement to keep everyone at their top performance. That includes you, too.

Regroup your teams and set them back to Recon mode before continuing. Use the UAV to scan the area to the south near the objective location, which holds several enemies. In addition to some gunners, there are soldiers armed with gun cameras, which allow them to fire at you without exposing themselves. Once you have detected these enemies, let the UAV return to high altitude and continue to monitor the area.

**Engage the enemies near the large building to the south.**

**Get those gunners on the rooftop.**

Move both of your teams with you as you advance down the walkway to the northwest of the building where the enemies are. Place the teams in positions of cover. The enemy will see you, so switch your troops' ROE to Assault and let them start firing. While keeping one team at this end, move along with the other through the covered walkway to the east to try to hit some of the hostiles from a different side. Assign targets for your team and also kill enemies on your own. Take out the gunners on the roof as soon as possible since their height advantage negates some of the effectiveness of your cover. Once all of the hostiles in this area have been eliminated, lead both of your teams to the objective location.

# 2. SECURE THE WATER FACILITY

MAP SECTION B

## Orders

Secure the two parts of the water facility.

## Secondary Objective

Neutralize fleeing vehicle.

**Advance toward the holding pools.**

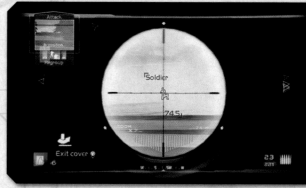

**The mist in the air decreases visibility. However, with the UAV monitoring overhead, you can use the intel markers on your HUD for targeting.**

The next objective is to secure the two parts of the water facility. Start off with the area to the southeast, where the water holding pools are. As usual, scan the area with the UAV to locate as many hostiles as possible. Watch for those on the rooftop and those around the pools. Order your teams to take positions behind walls or the large metal tanks next to the pools. Once they are in position, order both teams to Assault mode to start attacking. Add your fire to the mix and try to move around to the east, rushing from cover to cover, to hit the hostiles from their flank. As you clear the area, use the CFV for each team to order it to advance to the next cover. Your forces slowly move in on the building.

THE CAMPAIGN

Move your teams to the building.

**Throw frags over the pipes to take out the hostiles on the other side.**

Once the pool area is clear, move your teams up to the building. Check inside to make sure it is clear, then get ready to head up the walkway. Before doing so, send the UAV in for a last-second scan of the rooftop. There may be two or three hostiles up there waiting to ambush you. Now that you know their location, you can move and take cover behind the large concrete pipes on the roof. Position your teams behind the pipes as well and begin attacking. The enemies can be tough to kill behind cover, so use frag grenades to kill them if necessary.

**You don't have much time to shoot down the fleeing helicopter, so be ready.**

After the last hostile in this section has been neutralized, an enemy helicopter tries to escape. It approaches from the northwest and flies right over your position. Order your Ghost team (including the grenadier) to attack it and try to shoot it down as a secondary objective.

**These enemies attack you near the central part of this area.**

It is time to head toward the second objective location and secure it. As you advance northwest through the center of this area, which was previously clear, there are several hostiles. Take cover along with your team behind planters and kill these enemies.

Approach the western building from the east, using the buildings and objects for cover as you clear out the yard area.

The building at the area's western end is your objective. Approach it from the east, using the smaller buildings for cover, and scan it with the UAV to locate the hostiles around and on top of the building. Position one team to the southeast, the second to the east, and then also come in from the east yourself. Stacks of lumber and crates work for cover. Clear out the enemies in the yard south of the building and those you can see on the roof.

**Move inside the building and clear out the enemies.**

**Lead a team to the rooftop to eliminate any remaining hostiles.**

Once the outside is clear, move into the building. Order your teams to the corners near the doorway, then send them inside to take cover. A few hostiles lurk to the east, and hostiles on the roof shoot down through the skylights. Take cover behind the loading dock and clear out most of these enemies. One or two remain on the rooftop. Lead your Ghost team up the ramp to the roof while ordering your other team to stay below and cover the entrances to the building in case you missed someone outside. After killing the enemies on the roof, you receive new orders.

# 3. DISABLE JAMMER DEVICE

MAP SECTION C

## Orders

Reach and neutralize the jammer device on the building next to the dam.

**Take out those hostiles in the small building north of the dam.**

Intel indicates that the nukes are not at this facility. Instead, a top secret installation under the dam is the mercenaries' target. They are trying to hack into the U.S. missile defense system, and the Ghosts have to stop them. The objective is to the south across the dam. You must make it to the rooftop of that building and use an EMP (electromagnetic pulse) device on the jammer.

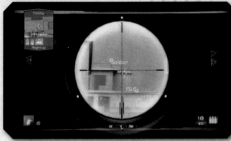

It is a long-range shot for an assault rifle, but you can kill one of the enemies on the rooftop of the large building south of the dam from the yard near the water facility building.

Lead your teams to the ground floor of the building, but do not rush out just yet. Send the UAV to scan the area around the dam. There are a couple of hostiles in the building on the north end of the dam, a few patrolling the dam, and lots on and in the building on the dam's south end.

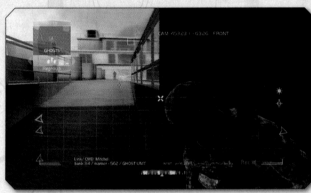

**Move your teams so they can cover the top of the dam and the walkway along the eastern side.**

Position your teams on the sides of the southern doorway so they locate the enemy in the small building to the south. As they open fire, move out and take cover behind some of the crates or pipes so you can take aim and shoot the hostiles through the window of the building where they are positioned. Lead your Ghost team into the building while you order the other team to take cover behind some crates to the building's east so they can cover the side of the dam.

If you get low on ammo for your primary weapon, pick up another from a dead enemy. The 36K Carbine is a very good weapon and will serve you well.

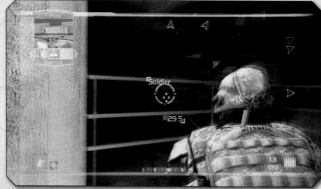

**Advance across the dam, taking out hostiles as they appear.**

Watch for enemies coming down the stairs.

Watch for enemies firing at you from the upper-level windows.

**Pick up a grenade launcher or light machine gun on your way to the roof.**

If hostiles try to take cover down this ramp at the end of the dam, throw a frag grenade in on them.

Eliminate all enemies on the rooftop.

   Position the Ghost team at the doorway leading out onto the dam and switch both teams to Assault mode. Help them clear the top of the dam so you can advance across it. Be sure to send your Ghosts to a position of cover behind the low concrete walls and move out yourself. Bring the other team out onto the dam as well. As you move across the dam, hostiles in the large building to the south fire at you from the upper floors. Take them out while staying behind cover. Order your teams to attack them. Advance across the dam in rushes, one team at a time, until you have made it across and cleared the dam in the process.

   It is time to enter the building. Lead your teams inside and watch for enemies coming down the stairs. Position the Army team to cover the stairs and send the Ghosts up ahead of you to scout for hostiles. The rest of the building should be clear, with the last enemies on the rooftop. However, before heading up, notice there are some weapons next to crates on each floor. You can find an M-32 MGL grenade launcher and an MG21 light machine gun. Pick up the grenade launcher and switch to your secondary weapon before heading up to the roof. Either a shotgun or submachine gun will do fine for clearing out remaining hostiles.

Place the EMP on the jammer and then get back.

Bring both teams up to the rooftop and order them to stay by the stairs while you walk over to the jammer device. Place an EMP charge on the device just like you would a C4 charge, then move away. It will detonate by timer and neutralize the jammer. It also knocks out your UAV.

# 4. DESTROY ENEMY HELICOPTERS

## MAP SECTION C

### Orders

Shoot down the two enemy helicopters that attack you.

The grenade launcher works well for shooting down the two choppers.

As soon as the jammer is down, bring your Ghost team to the roof and order it behind cover. A couple of enemy helicopters are inbound. One is a Havoc, the other an Mi-17. Switch to the grenade launcher you picked up and start shooting at the choppers. Order

your Ghost team to attack as well. The grenadier should assist. You need to get in a few hits to bring down each helicopter. The key is to keep moving so you are not an easy target. You only have 12 rounds in your grenade launcher, so if you run out before both helicopters are down, run down the stairs to pick up another grenade launcher or the light machine gun.

## TIP

If the helicopter is at medium distance, aim a bit above it so the grenade will still hit it as it flies in an arc-shaped path.

# 5. REACH EXTRACTION POINT

## MAP SECTION D

### Orders

Advance to the extraction zone with your teams.

Move west to the other building as you make your way to the extraction point.

After the helicopter threat has been neutralized, lead your teams back down the stairs to the lower level of the building and advance west to another building. From there you can descend to the convoy along the road, which is waiting to take you to the final mission in the campaign. The nuke is still in play.

The convoy is waiting for you.

## TIP

Before heading to the extraction point, be sure to pick up an assault rifle; you are moving to the next mission right away and won't have time to change out for something else.

THE CAMPAIGN

# Just Shut Up and Do Your Job

## GRAW2 ▶ SINGLE PLAYER
### MISSION 12: WHO THE HELL ARE THESE GUYS?

**OBJECTIVES**

**OBJECTIVE 1**
SECURE THE ZONE.

**OBJECTIVE 2**
HOLD YOUR POSITION.

**OBJECTIVE 3**
REACH GHOST TRUCK FOR RESUPPLY.

**OBJECTIVE 4**
CROSS THE BRIDGE AND THEN THE BORDER.

**OBJECTIVE 5**
FIND NBC THREAT.

**OBJECTIVE 6**
DESTROY NBC WEAPON.

## LEGEND

- ◉ = Insertion Point
- ◎ = Extraction Point
- **Gt** = Ghost Truck
- **R** = Rifleman (Soldats)
- **G** = Machine Gunner (Soldats)
- **A** = Antitank (Soldats)
- **Gf** = Machine Gun Fixed (Soldats)
- **M** = Mowag (Soldats)
- **P** = Panhard (Soldats)

## OBJECTIVES

1. Secure the border.
2. Hold position.
3. Move to rally point.
4. Cross the border.
5. Find and neutralize the nuke.

## MISSION BRIEFING

PUENTE CORDOVA
US/MEXICAN BORDER

The Humvee takes you to the Mexican border.

The mercenaries have hacked a top secret military data storage facility and managed to weaken the Missile Shield protecting the United States: Los Angeles, Chicago, New York, even Washington could be hit. Your mission is to locate and neutralize the last nuke.

## 1. SECURE THE BORDER

### MAP SECTION A

### Orders

Neutralize the enemy positions at the border.

**Destroy the Mowag.**

**Change positions or advance with your team to clear out all of the enemies near the parking lot.**

Watch for a Mowag APC to approach. As soon as you see it, order your team to take it out. If it approaches the eastern end of the parking lot, it will drop off more enemy riflemen. Once there are no more enemies that you can engage from your location, order your team to advance to the end of the parking lot and hold behind cover. Check for any hostiles that might be hiding behind wrecked cars or other objects.

**You take enemy fire as soon as the mission begins. Get your team and yourself behind cover.**

This mission continues right after the last one. You begin with the same Ghost team and weapons with which you ended the previous mission. As you step out of the Humvee, you come under fire from mercenaries to the east. Quickly take cover behind anything you can before you get hit.

**Kill those gunners on the rooftop.**

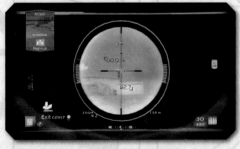

**Head up the hill and position your team along this wall.**

Make sure your teammates are behind cover, and change the ROE to Assault so they will engage the enemy on their own. There are more mercenaries on and around a building at the top of the hill east of the parking lot where you are positioned. Kill the gunners on the roof since they will try to keep your team pinned.

## TIP

The stacks of concrete blocks can be shot away by sustained fire from the enemy gunners, so don't stay behind them for too long or you will end up without cover.

**Watch out for this hostile to the right side of the building.**

Lead your team up the hill to the building. Position the Ghosts along the left corner of the wall while you take the right corner. Use caution; a hostile lurks behind the planters off to the right of your position. Be sure to locate and neutralize him before moving any farther. Use the CFV of your Ghosts to give them targets to attack. Then advance east along the building's southern wall so you can hit from the flank the hostiles your team is attacking.

**Hit the enemies from the side.**

**Take out the Panhard or it will keep driving around as it shoots up your team.**

With the area around the building clear, move your team to a position south of the building, behind some planters. There may still be one or two hostiles on the rooftop who will try to hit you as you advance toward the objective location. Kill them first. However, don't go too far yet. A Panhard is on the way to engage you before you can go anywhere. Order your team to attack it while you shoot the gunner and eliminate the vehicle as a threat.

**Head north to the checkpoint.**

Now advance to the border checkpoint. Order your team to regroup on your position and switch the ROE back to Recon. Move quickly to the concrete wall and position your team behind it for cover. If the enemy has already seen you and opened fire, switch your team to Assault mode immediately. However, if you make it down to this area undetected, let your team detect as many hostiles as possible before letting it loose to attack.

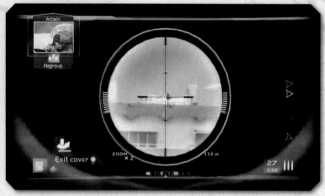

**The fixed machine gun on the rooftop should be your first target.**

Move to the corner of the wall and peek around to begin engaging hostiles. The main threat is the machine gun on the rooftop. Use your scope to line up a shot, and take out the gunner. Keep watching the gun because more hostiles will move to man it. Pick targets for your team and hold by the concrete wall until all enemies you can detect have been eliminated.

**There are more hostiles to the southeast.**

When it looks clear, order your team to advance in Recon mode and take cover behind either the concrete barricades or the back of the black semitrailer. A few more hostiles await to the southeast on the opposite side of the border checkpoint. Take them out.

# 2. HOLD POSITION

**MAP SECTION B**

## Orders

Hold the position on the U.S. side of the bridge over the border and engage any mercenaries trying to cross.

Move forward to man the machine guns.

Order your team to move behind one sandbag position. Once there, order it to man the gun.

Lead your Ghosts to the sandbag positions and order them to man one of the M50 machine guns while you take control of the second M50. Your new objective is to defend this location and prevent mercenaries from crossing the border. Make sure your team is in Assault mode, and get ready to use the machine gun to take on waves of enemies.

Destroy the Panhard driving across the bridge to attack you.

Aim for the cars the hostiles are taking cover behind.

A Panhard drives across the bridge first along the left lane. Open fire on the vehicle and destroy it if you can get a shot. Otherwise, order your team to destroy it. Now turn your attention to the enemy infantry. They will take cover behind cars on the bridge—not a smart idea. Rather than targeting the soldiers individually, fire at the car they are using for cover. When it explodes, the hostiles die. Another Panhard comes at you along the right lane of the road. Neutralize it and any remaining infantry. Finally, some tanks and a helicopter move in to secure the border.

Other U.S. forces move in to protect the border.

# 3. MOVE TO RALLY POINT

**MAP SECTION B**

## Orders

Advance with your team to the Ghost truck for resupply.

The Ghost truck waits for you at the rally point.

PRIMA OFFICIAL GAME GUIDE

114

The border is now secure. Lead your team to the rally point, where you can get ready for the final part of the mission. For your team, select the grenadier and the combat medic to go along with your rifleman. The enemy up ahead has a lot of firepower, and it is always nice to have a medic to care for wounds you and your team may suffer. Select a large-caliber assault rifle, such as the M468, SCAR-H, or even Rx4 Storm, and the offensive pack of grenades. Take a submachine gone for your secondary weapon. You can use some frags for the rest of the mission.

This tank is now under your command.

You have been given command of a couple of support assets. An M1A2 main battle tank will provide your heavy firepower. You also have a Littlebird attack helicopter for air cover and to keep an eye on the sky. Both will come in real handy as you engage a lot of hostiles.

# 4. CROSS THE BORDER

MAP SECTION B

## Orders

Lead your forces across the bridge into Mexico.

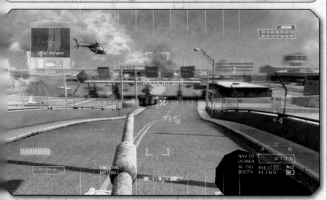

Use the CFV to give orders to your tank.

Your next job is to move your team and support across the border into Mexico. Order the Littlebird to fly to a position over the checkpoint on the Mexican side of the border while sending your tank forward as well. Lead your team in behind the tank. The Littlebird will detect enemies ahead for you, including a Mowag APC.

Bring your team forward to the border checkpoint.

Use the CFV for the tank to target the Mowag so the tank will fire on it and destroy this first main threat. Continue advancing with your teammates and order them to take cover behind the concrete barriers at the checkpoint. Set their ROE to Assault and they will start attacking on their own. You can use your rifle to take out enemies, but you have some heavy support, so use it.

The Littlebird is a great asset for attacking both vehicles and infantry.

Move your tank forward to deal with a Panhard and other Mowags that show up. Also use the CFV for the Littlebird. You can move the camera around and order the chopper to attack not only vehicles, but also soldiers behind cover. When you give the Littlebird a target, it automatically moves into position to attack it. Keep up the attacks until all enemies in this area have been eliminated.

## TIP

You do not even need your team or your own rifle to neutralize the enemies on the Mexican side of the border. Just use your CFV for the M1A2 tank and the Littlebird to sight targets, then give both movement and attack orders.

# 5. FIND AND NEUTRALIZE THE NUKE

## MAP SECTION C

### Orders

Localize the nuke and then target the missile launcher.

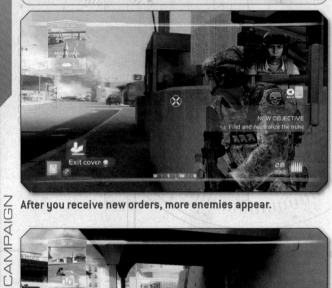

**After you receive new orders, more enemies appear.**

**Advance south into Mexico.**

After you receive your new orders, more hostiles move in from the west to attack. Keep your Littlebird over the street south of the border checkpoint since there are some anti-tank gunners farther west. Use the copter and the tank to take out any vehicles that approach while you lead your team south from the checkpoint to take cover behind the building.

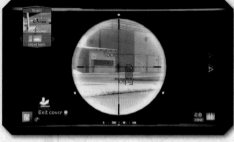

**Kill this anti-tank gunner so you can move your tank in for support.**

While your team stays on the northern corner to engage enemies near the warehouse to the west, move along the building's wall to the southern corner. Peek around to locate an anti-tank gunner. He is over 100 meters away, so use your scope and take him out. You can then move your tank forward a bit. Stop it as it makes the turn to the west and advances even with the building where you are located.

**Move your team toward the warehouse.**

Along with your team, neutralize any hostiles around the warehouse, then advance quickly across the open space. Order your team to take cover behind the loading dock while you move up the ramp to the edge of the doorway and help clear out any remaining enemies in the warehouse.

THE CAMPAIGN

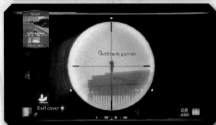

Position your team by the door and then take out the anti-tank gunner on the rooftop.

Move in the tank to take out the rest.

When it is clear, move your team in to take cover to the side of the doorway in the western wall of the warehouse while you move behind a stack of lumber. Your main target here is the anti-tank gunner on the roof of the Chemex building to the west. Once he has been taken out, stay behind cover and move the tank forward. By this time, the Littlebird has been called away; however, the tank is all you need. As before, use the CFV to give the tank attack orders, and it can clear out the remainder of hostiles all by itself. Move the tank a bit at a time—just enough to get a line of fire on the next enemy. Continue advancing the tank until it reaches the end of its movement, where it will continue to provide covering fire for your team.

Be ready for hostiles to come down these stairs.

Now that all of the enemies by the Chemex building have been killed, order your team to regroup on you and move west toward the stairs. Place your team behind cover to the east of the stairs and keep it in Assault mode. As you approach the stairs, some hostiles come down to try to flank you. Your team should take care of them—but give attack orders if necessary.

Take cover here and start taking out mercenaries.

Quickly head upstairs and take cover behind a group of barrels, then order your team to move to cover behind a wall northeast of your position. Several hostiles to the north fire down on your position. If necessary, throw a smoke grenade so your team can move into position. Along with your team, eliminate these enemies. Don't forget that you have frag grenades, which can be useful if the hostiles stay hidden behind cover.

Kill those hostiles on the rooftop.

Now that you have located the launchers, an air strike is inbound. However, the pilots need you to target the launchers for them. Order your team to take cover to the south while you move to the building's edge. Select the air support in your Cross-Com, line up one of the launchers in your reticle, and call in the strike.

**The nukes have been neutralized.**

Since you had to stay close to target the missile launchers, you were hit by the blast. However, you succeeded in your mission, prevented the mercenaries from launching a nuclear weapon at the United States, and saved millions of citizens—who will never even know what you and the Ghosts have done for them.

**Shoot down that chopper!**

Once this immediate area is clear, lead your team up the stairs and take cover behind two groups of barrels. There are more hostiles on the rooftop of a building to the north and down by the missile launchers below. However, your main threat is an Mi-17 helicopter that appears and attacks you. Order your team to destroy the helicopter. Your grenadier should be able to get some hits on it. Add your firepower and try to take out the gunner in the door of the chopper so you won't have to endure any fire from it. Keep up the pressure until you shoot down this threat.

**Good job, soldier!. The campaign is complete.**

**Target the launchers for an air strike.**

# Multiplayer

# Warfare in the 21st Century

*Tom Clancy's Ghost Recon: Advanced Warfighter 2* for the Xbox 360 offers complete multiplayer gameplay—both online (via Xbox Live) and offline, in which gamers share the same screen or connect multiple Xbox 360 consoles together via System Link. Whether you're wading online and clashing against next-gen soldiers from around the world or you're battling a buddy on the couch next to you, you will find a host of different game types. Deathmatch purists can always lean toward Sharpshooter matches. Feeling less than adversarial? Try out co-op missions, where you work together to ward off AI-controlled terrorists.

The multiplayer game offers a variety of different elements and enhancements. Not every soldier enters the fray on the same footing. Players can choose between different soldier classes to suit their gameplay style. Expert snipers may gravitate toward the Marksman class, while players more inclined to blow things up may select Grenadier class. You can alter the appearance of your soldier so you stand out against other players on the battlefield.

As with any battle, advance intelligence is a key element to success. Study the included maps to get pre-op know-how, like the most effective sniper points and the best routes for getting unarmed officers to safety in Escort missions. Familiarity with both the lay of the land and the firepower you must use to wrest control of the territory from the enemy goes a long way when trying to increase your online ranking.

To play *Tom Clancy's Ghost Recon: Advanced Warfighter 2* online, you must have an active Xbox Live account. Please see the Xbox 360 manual for instructions on how to set up and maintain your Xbox Live account, or visit www.xbox.com/connect for more information.

Multiplayer games are not limited to Xbox Live subscribers. All game modes can be played via split-screen gameplay (players share a screen divided into two or four portions) or System Link. System Link requires one Xbox 360 system and television per player. An Ethernet cable or home network connection (such as a router) is required to link the consoles.

# Identity

While all soldiers fight for the same cause—victory—each player can set up an individual identity in order to look different from the other soldiers in the field. Identity comprises three factors: Class, Head Gear, and Face. The Head Gear and Face categories are only cosmetic alterations, but your selected class can have serious bearing on your performance on the battlefield.

To complete your identity, you can also select a default class for multiplayer games, as well as the default gear you want to use for each of the four different classes. This customization makes playing a game very quick. Take some time to choose the weapons you like best for each class. Then, during the setup phase of a multiplayer game, you can either go with your default class and be ready to go or just switch to a different class; your choice of weapons and equipment for that class will be automatically selected. If desired, you can always change weapons when you begin a game.

# The Classes

There are four soldier classes, each with its own strengths. Benefits include additional ammunition and faster reload rates for certain weapons—which are listed with each class—and higher accuracy with preferred weapons in specific situations.

You can change your class as often as you like before going into battle. You can also select a default class you always occupy unless you specifically make a class change.

## NOTE

None of the class strengths or talents come at the expense of another talent. Just because the marksman is especially lethal with a sniper rifle does not mean that the Marksman class is below average with other gear, such as grenades. It just means that the marksman is as good with other weapons and ordnance as the other classes that do not enjoy class-specific gear bonuses.

## RIFLEMAN

Riflemen-class players excel at medium- and close-quarters combat and are best utilized as the forward element of any effective team. Riflemen have increased accuracy with all weapons from an upright position, allowing them to fire more effectively while on the move. Players using this class also have increased skills and benefits when using Rifleman-class weapons, such as a general increase in accuracy, quicker reload times, and more magazines. Riflemen make good all-around soldiers because they don't receive penalties for using weapons outside of their class.

RIFLEMAN WEAPONS: Cx4 Storm, Cx4 Storm SD, MR-C, MP5SD, SR-3, Rx4 Storm, Rx4 Storm SD, A4 Rifle, M-556, 36K Carbine, SCAR-L Carbine, SCAR-LCQC, AG A3, SA-80, FAMAS, AK-74SU, T-95, M468, M468 SD, AK-47, SCAR-H SV, MK14 EBR

## GRENADIER

Grenadier-class players are at their best using area-of-effect fire to eliminate groups of enemies and enemies behind cover. They are also particularly effective against vehicle threats. Grenadier bonuses include greater accuracy with launched grenades, more ammunition, and quicker reloads for Grenadier-class weapons. Grenadiers are less effective with Automatic Rifleman— and Marksman-class weapons.

GRENADIER WEAPONS: Cx4 Storm/XL6, MR-C/AGL, Rx4 Storm/XL7, A4 Rifle/M320, M-556/M320, SCAR-L/EGLM, SCAR-LCQC/EGLM, AG A3/SGL, SA-80/M320, FAMAS/M204, T-95/M320, M468/M320, M468 SD/M320, M-32 MGL, M-32 MGL Smoke, Zeus MPAR

## AUTOMATIC RIFLEMAN

Automatic Rifleman–class players' primary role is to provide suppressive fire on key choke points and enemy positions. An effectively positioned automatic rifleman can cut off key areas of the map by pouring down fire while teammates of other classes flank the suppressed position. Automatic riflemen have increased accuracy with all weapons while firing fully automatic as well as increased accuracy in the crouched and prone positions. Automatic riflemen are less effective with Marksman-class weapons.

AUTOMATIC RIFLEMAN WEAPONS: A556 SAW, M36 SAW, T-95 LMG, AK-47 LMG, MG21, M60, MK48 LMG

## MARKSMAN

Marksman-class players excel at providing long-range, accurate, and direct fire to support the forward elements of their team. An effective marksman takes the environment into account, locating the best cover to remain concealed. Marksmen have increased accuracy with all weapons when firing in single-shot mode or from the prone position. When using a Marksman-class weapon, marksmen have additional increased accuracy and the ability to more quickly stabilize their weapon for quick, successive shots. Marksmen are less effective firing any weapon on full automatic.

MARKSMAN WEAPONS: VSK-50 Sniper, SR A550, M107 Sniper, SR 25 Sniper, SR 25 SD Sniper, SVD Sniper, KJY-88 Sniper, M-556 SL

# APPEARANCES

Before going into a multiplayer game, you can change your soldier's face and head gear. None of these options affect your soldier's skills—they are purely cosmetic ways of customizing your soldier's appearance. You can select different appearances for each of the four classes so you look the part when you play as a marksman or a grenadier.

## FACE SELECTION

Female Face 1 | Female Face 2 | Female Face 3 | Female Face 4 | Female Face 5 | Female Face 6 | Female Face 7

Female Face 8 | Female Face 9 | Female Face 10 | Male Face 1 | Male Face 2 | Male Face 3 | Male Face 4

Male Face 5 | Male Face 6 | Male Face 7 | Male Face 8 | Male Face 9 | Male Face 10

## HEAD GEAR

 **IWH 2011 B 1: Artisent Integrated Warfighter Helmet 2011 B with Oakley Tactical A Frame Goggles**

 **IWH 2011 B 2: Artisent Integrated Warfighter Helmet 2011 B with SWD Goggles**

 **IWH 2011 B 3: Artisent Integrated Warfighter Helmet 2011 B**

IWH 2011 B 4: Artisent Integrated Warfighter Helmet 2011 B with Mandible and Tactical Eyewear

IWH 2011 B 5: Artisent Integrated Warfighter Helmet 2011 B with Mandible

IWH 2011 B 6: Artisent Integrated Warfighter Helmet 2011 B with CRBN Mask and Mandible

IWH 2013 CRBN 1: Crye Associates Integrated Warfighter Helmet 2013 B with CRBN Mask Ballistic Lens Down

IWH 2013 CRBN 2: Crye Associates Integrated Warfighter Helmet 2013 B with CRBN Mask Ballistic Lens Up

IWH 2012 1: Artisent Integrated Warfighter Helmet 2012

IWH 2012 2: Artisent Integrated Warfighter Helmet 2012 with Oakley Tactical A Frame Goggles

Red Storm Cap: Red Storm Cap with TCI Tactical Assault Communications Headset

Ops-Core Cap

TCI Cap: Tactical Command Industries Cap

Crye Precision Cap

Blackhawk Products Group Cap

ICS-PL Helmet: Rainbow Six Vegas Team Helmet with Integrated Communications System and Protective Lens

PASGT Helmet: PASGT Helmet with Face Mask and BlackHawk Special Operations Tactical Goggles

Bandana 1: OD Bandana with Oakley M Frame Eyewear

Bandana 2: OD Bandana with TCI Tactical Assault Communications Headset

Boonie Hat 1: Crye Precision Boonie Hat

Boonie Hat 2: Crye Precision Boonie Hat with TCI Tactical Assault Communications Headset

Boonie Hat 3: Crye Precision Boonie Hat with Tactical Eyewear

Field Cap 1: Crye Precision Field Cap with TCI Liberator II Tactical Headset

Field Cap 2: Crye Precision Field Cap with Oakley M Frame Eyewear and TCI Patrol II Tactical Headset

Liberator: TCI Liberator II Tactical Headset

ACH Helmet 1: ACH Helmet

ACH Helmet 2: ACH Helmet with Oakley Tactical A Frame Goggles and TCI Liberator II Tactical Headset

ACH Helmet 3: ACH Helmet with BlackHawk Special Operations Tactical Goggles and TCI Patrol II Tactical Headset

ACH Helmet 4: ACH Helmet with SWD Goggles and TCI Tactical Assault Communications Headset

ACH Helmet 5: ACH Helmet with Tactical Eyewear

ACH Covered 1: ACH Helmet with Crye Precision Cover

ACH Covered 2: ACH Helmet with Crye Precision Cover, Hatch B.O.S.S. 6000 Tactical Eye Protection, and TCI Liberator II Tactical Headset

ACH Covered 3: ACH Helmet with Crye Precision Cover and Oakley Tactical O Frame Goggles

ACH Covered 4: ACH Helmet with Crye Precision Cover and TCI Patrol II Tactical Headset

Oakley Cap: Oakley Cap with Oakley M Frame Eyewear

MSA Paraclete Helmet 1: MSA Paraclete Attack Helmet

MSA Paraclete Helmet 2: MSA Paraclete Attack Helmet with Oakley Tactical A Frame Goggles

MSA Paraclete Helmet 3: MSA Paraclete Attack Helmet with Hatch B.O.S.S. 6000 Tactical Eye Protection

MSA Paraclete Helmet 4: MSA Paraclete Attack Helmet with Oakley M Frame Eyewear

MSA Paraclete Helmet 5: MSA Paraclete Attack Helmet with Tactical Eyewear

MSA Paraclete Cap: MSA Paraclete Cap with Tactical Eyewear

Patrol Cap 1: Patrol Cap

Patrol Cap 2: Patrol Cap with Oakley M Frame Eyewear

Safariland Cap: Safariland Cap with TCI Tactical Assault Communications Headset

Mich 2001 Helmet 1: MICH 2001 Helmet with TCI Liberator Tactical Headset

 **Mich 2001 Helmet 2:** MICH 2001 Helmet with SWD Goggles and TCI Tactical Assault Communication Headset

 **Mich 2001 Helmet 3:** MICH 2001 Helmet with Tactical Eyewear and TCI Tactical Assault Communication Headset

 **HeatGear Hood 1:** Under Armour Tactical HeatGear Hood

 **HeatGear Hood 2:** Under Armour Tactical HeatGear Hood with Oakley Tactical A Frame Goggles

 **Blackhawk Watch Cap 1:** BlackHawk Hell Storm Low Profile Fleece Watch Cap

 **Blackhawk Watch Cap 2:** BlackHawk Hell Storm Low Profile Fleece Watch Cap with TCI Tactical Assault Communications Headset

# XBOX 360 ACHIEVEMENTS FOR MULTIPLAYER

Achievements are recognitions earned by completing in-game requirements and are visible to other players from your Xbox Live profile. The more achievements you earn, the higher your overall Gamer Score, which many players wear as a badge of honor. *Tom Clancy's Ghost Recon: Advanced Warfighter 2* has 22 achievements for multiplayer games that are awarded by completing goals, such as a specific number of headshots.

## MULTIPLAYER ACHIEVEMENTS

| Achievement | Requirement | Gamer Score Points |
|---|---|---|
| Team Veteran | Win 30 team matches with at least 5 gamertags in the room. | 25 |
| Solo Veteran | Win 10 solo matches with at least 5 gamertags in the room. | 25 |
| Ultimate Defender | Win a 60-minute co-op Defend match on any map. | 40 |
| Helo Hunter | Shoot down 20 helicopters in the Helicopter Hunt game type. | 20 |
| Demo Expert | Plant 10 demo charges in Team Mission matches with at least 5 gamertags in the room. | 20 |
| Combat Medic | Heal 10 teammates wounded by enemy fire in a multiplayer match with at least 5 gamertags in the room. | 25 |
| Team MVP | Lead your team in kills in a team match with at least 5 gamertags on your team. | 15 |
| Team All-Star | Lead your team in kills in 10 team matches with at least 5 gamertags on your team. | 35 |
| Enforcer | Eliminate 5 different human opponents in 30 seconds with at least 10 gamertags in the room. | 20 |
| Threatening | Get a total of 50 kills in team or solo matches with at least 5 gamertags in the room. | 10 |
| Dangerous | Get a total of 150 kills in team or solo matches with at least 5 gamertags in the room. | 15 |

| Achievement | Requirement | Gamer Score Points |
|---|---|---|
| Lethal | Get a total of 300 kills in team or solo matches with at least 5 gamertags in the room. | 20 |
| Ruthless | Get a total of 500 kills in team or solo matches with at least 5 gamertags in the room. | 25 |
| Sniper Expert | Get a total of 100 sniper rifle kills in team or solo matches with at least 5 gamertags in the room. | 20 |

## CO-OP ACHIEVEMENTS

| Achievement | Requirement | Gamer Score Points |
|---|---|---|
| Station (Co-op 1) Perfect | Complete co-op campaign mission without failing an objective, with no respawns, on default or hard. | 20 |
| The Cut (Co-op 2) Perfect | Complete co-op campaign mission without failing an objective, with no respawns, on default or hard. | 20 |
| Locks (Co-op 3) Perfect | Complete co-op campaign mission without failing an objective, with no respawns, on default or hard. | 20 |
| Caldera (Co-op 4) Perfect | Complete co-op campaign mission without failing an objective, with no respawns, on default or hard. | 20 |
| Outpost (Co-op 5) Perfect | Complete co-op campaign mission without failing an objective, with no respawns, on default or hard. | 20 |
| Hideout (Co-op 6) Perfect | Complete co-op campaign mission without failing an objective, with no respawns, on default or hard. | 20 |
| Perfect Co-op Campaign | Complete all co-op campaign missions without failing an objective, with no respawns, on default or hard. | 40 |
| Co-op Veteran | Win 30 co-op matches with at least 5 gamertags in the room. | 25 |

# Game Modes and Types

*Tom Clancy's Ghost Recon: Advanced Warfighter 2* includes a great number and variety of multiplayer game modes and match types, from team-based contests over real estate to cooperative missions that force players to work in an alliance to overcome a sophisticated, AI-controlled enemy. For those who like a deathmatch, there is also the Sharpshooter mode.

There are 12 game modes, with a few game types within each. Once you select the game mode, you select the type, which details the specific parameters of action and the necessary requirements for victory. If you want to test your skills in more than the included game types, multiple customization tools within each mode let you decide the factors for a successful match.

## CAMPAIGN MODE

In Campaign mode, all players square off against AI-controlled forces. The goal is to complete a series of mission objectives before the time is up or before all players are eliminated in the field. The only match type in Campaign mode is Mission, which places soldiers in a direct combat situation with a series of primary and secondary objectives (such as heading off enemy reinforcements or gathering intel on enemy activities).

Campaign players must not only make mission objectives a priority, but also work together and constantly communicate to keep each other alive. There are no respawns in this mode—once you have been neutralized, you must watch the rest of the battle from the sidelines. If you are playing online, keep chatter limited to mission-specific intel. With so much happening at once, a solid chain of command is a good idea, so all orders are routed through a single player.

## CO-OP ELIMINATION MODE

Co-op Elimination mode mobilizes all players into a single tactical unit and charges them with flushing out and neutralizing enemies spread around the map. With the singular

focus of dispatching enemy threats, players are able to take greater liberties with their in-game tactics. Still, communication always trumps bravado when victory is on the line. Whenever an enemy is spotted, players should alert all other players of the enemy's location. If there are too many targets for one player to handle, backup must be requested.

There are two match types in Co-op Elimination mode: Firefight and Helicopter Hunt. You must hunt down either enemy infantry or helicopters. You can also customize this mode so you have to deal with infantry and helicopters together.

## CO-OP TERRITORY MODE

Co-op Territory mode gathers all players into a single force to stop AI-controlled enemies from planting bombs at various zones on the map. The zones are noted on the charts for each available map. With multiple enemies making their demolition efforts in tandem, teamwork is imperative. While it may sound easy to muster all available soldiers and squeeze each terrorist bomber squad one by one, you can ill afford to let even a single bomb be activated.

The only match type for this mode is Defend. The value of life is at a premium, with absolutely no respawns available to players. Once you are out, you must spectate for the rest of the match. Players win by neutralizing all enemies, preventing them from planting any bombs, and having at least one soldier survive the end of the match.

# CO-OP OBJECTIVE MODE

Co-op Objective mode enlists all players for duty on a single team. The goal is to infiltrate specific zones on the map and avoid enemy detection. There are three types in this mode: Intel Recon, Recon, and Stealth Recon—all of which task players with gathering intel in different zones on the map while the enemy sends out regular patrols. Firefights are not advised, as they raise alarm and attract reinforcements. Since players cannot respawn after being killed, stealth is priority one.

# TEAM ELIMINATION MODE

Team Elimination mode splits the players into two warring factions with only one goal—complete elimination of the opposition. Soldiers must exercise teamwork if they are to successfully corner and neutralize the enemy team. Every kill equals a point, and the team with the most points at the end of the mode is the winner. There are three game types in Team Elimination. Sharpshooter matches end with the first team to reach 50 kills. All players have unlimited respawns. Last Man Standing matches, however, allow no respawns—the game ends when one team is completely wiped out or the time is up. In Takedown, there are infinite respawns and the winner is the team with the most points when the time runs out. However, one player from each team is designated as the officer and is worth more points than the rest of the team members when killed.

# TEAM TERRITORY MODE

Team Territory mode divides players into two groups and charges them with controlling specific zones on the available maps. Team Territory offers four match types: Domination, Hamburger Hill, Siege, and Blind Siege. The number of zones varies by type as well as how control is determined. In some, you must capture a zone, while in others you have to have one of your team occupy the zone to maintain control. A customization tool allows for drawing up host-preferred match parameters.

# TEAM OBJECTIVE MODE

Team Objective mode also splits the players into two opposing parties, but it then sends them out into the field to capture different points of interest on the map. This is another mode that requires deft teamwork and solid communication, as the objects in question are not plentiful. There are three match types for Team Objective: the traditional Capture the Flag, Recovery, and Search and Rescue. Hosts can also customize their own matches.

## TEAM BATTLE MODE

In this mode, teams must capture each of five zones and score points for control (as in the Battle type) or be the first to control all five zones simultaneously (as in the Divide and Conquer type). This mode requires the members of a team to coordinate their actions so they can capture zones and then maintain control of them. To make this mode more interesting, teams can receive AI infantry and helicopter reinforcements as they take control of zones, providing for much larger battles.

## TEAM MISSION MODE

Team Missions pit two teams against each other as they fight to complete competing mission objectives. There is only one type of game—Mission—where the Ghost team must place demo charges at three of the five zones and then reach an extraction point. The enemy team must stop them, and they have AI support to help them complete their task. This is a great attack vs. defend mode.

## SOLO ELIMINATION MODE

Solo Elimination mode includes traditional deathmatch-style gameplay and a few other match types that add wrinkles to the familiar formula. All games in this mode, though, are free-for-all firefights with all players looking out for themselves. Soldiers spawn into the map at random points, then seek out targets to earn points. There are several match types for Solo Elimination, including Last Man Standing and Sharpshooter as well as Bounty Hunter, Seek and Destroy, and Thief.

## SOLO TERRITORY MODE

Solo Territory is another free-for-all mode where soldiers compete not for kills, but for square footage. Players are certainly encouraged to hunt each other down, but you win only by occupying specific zones on the map to earn points. These games can be frenzied, especially if you are the soldier who occupies the sole contested piece of land. There are two game types for this mode—Hamburger Hill, which has only one zone, and Domination, with five zones. Hosts can also use a customization tool to create unique matches.

MULTIPLAYER

# SOLO OBJECTIVE MODE

Solo Objective mode games strip away teamwork and force players to look out for number one. The goal in these games is to seek out an objective (such as a flag or an officer) and hold onto it for points while the other players hunt him or her down without mercy. Players that manage to successfully acquire objects of interest are encouraged to make themselves scarce, as all players in the match are made aware of a met objective. There are two match types for Solo Objective—Flag Carry and Escort—as well as a customization tool.

## QUICK REFERENCE FOR GAME MODES AND TYPES

| Mode | Types Available | Description |
|---|---|---|
| Campaign | Mission | Play a campaign mission where players must defeat enemy forces and complete objectives to win. Respawns are off. |
| Co-op Elimination | Firefight | Players must eliminate a large enemy force. The team wins when all enemies have been eliminated. Each player has three respawns; all players are on one team. |
| | Helicopter Hunt | Players must survive against multiple waves of enemy helicopters. |
| Co-op Territory | Defend | Players must prevent enemy forces from planting bombs at various zones. The team wins when all enemies are eliminated or when the time expires. No respawns. |
| Co-op Objective | Intel Recon | Players must retrieve intel from each of five zones and return it to their insertion point while enemy forces patrol the area. The team wins when all intel has been successfully retrieved. No respawns. |
| | Recon | Players must recon each of five zones while enemy forces patrol the area. The team wins when all five zones have been successfully scouted. No respawns. |
| | Stealth Recon | Players must recon each of five zones while enemy forces patrol the area. The team wins when all five zones have been successfully scouted. Points are deducted for each enemy killed. No respawns. |
| Team Elimination | Last Man Standing | Each team attempts to eliminate the other. The team with the most points when time is up wins. No respawns; players are on two teams. |
| | Sharpshooter | Each team attempts to eliminate the other, and players receive points for each kill. The first team to 50 points wins. Infinite respawns; players are on two teams. |
| | Takedown | Each team attempts to eliminate the other, and players receive points for each kill. A player on each team designated as the officer is worth more points when eliminated. Infinite respawns; players are on two teams. |

| Mode | Types Available | Description |
|---|---|---|
| Team Territory | Blind Siege | One team defends a random zone. The other team inserts at a random zone and must take the defending zone. No respawns; players are on two teams. |
| | Domination | Teams must capture each of five zones, and they score points for each zone they control. The team with the most points when time is up wins. Players get infinite respawns and are on two teams. |
| | Hamburger Hill | Get to the central zone and remain in it while keeping the enemy team out to score points. The team with the most points when time is up wins. Infinite respawns; players are on two teams. |
| | Siege | One team attempts to capture the other team's base. Whichever team eliminates the other, or owns the base when time is up, wins. No respawns; players are on two teams. |
| Team Objective | Capture the Flag | Each team attempts to retrieve a flag from the opposite base and return it to its own. A point is awarded for each capture. The first team to 10 wins. Infinite respawns; players are on two teams. |
| | Recovery | Teams must retrieve a single flag from a central zone and return it to their base. A point is awarded for each capture. The first team to 10 wins. Infinite respawns; players are on two teams. |
| | Search and Rescue | Teams must escort three unarmed officers back to their base. Teams score per second for each officer held. The team with the most points when time is up wins. Infinite respawns; players are on two teams. |
| Team Battle | Battle | Teams must capture each of five zones, and they score points for each zone they control. The first team to 1,500 points wins. Infinite respawns; players are on two teams. |
| | Divide and Conquer | Teams must capture each of five zones, and they score points for each zone they control. AI soldiers are given as reinforcements as zones are captured. The first team to hold all five zones at once wins. Infinite respawns; players are on two teams. |
| Team Mission | Mission | The Ghost team must place demo charges in three of the five enemy zones, then reach the extraction area. The enemy team must work with its AI support to stop the Ghosts. Five individual respawns are allowed; players are on two teams. |
| Solo Elimination | Bounty Hunter | Players receive incrementally higher points for consecutive target kills. Killing others resets points per kill. The player with the most points when time is up wins. Infinite respawns; each player is on his or her own. |
| | Last Man Standing | The player with the most kills when time is up or when only one player is left alive wins. No respawns; each player is on his or her own. |
| | Seek and Destroy | Score by eliminating and becoming the target, or by eliminating players as they become the target. The player with the most points when time is up wins. Infinite respawns; each player is on his or her own. |

| Mode | Types Available | Description |
|---|---|---|
| | Sharpshooter | The player with the most kills wins the round. Infinite respawns; each player is on his or her own. |
| | Thief | The player with the highest score becomes the thief. Score two points for killing the thief and one for other kills. The first player to 15 points wins. Infinite respawns; each player is on his or her own. |
| Solo Territory | Domination | Players work to capture five target zones, and they score points for each zone they control. The player with the most points when time is up wins the round. Infinite respawns; each player is on his or her own. |
| | Hamburger Hill | A single, central zone is the target, and a player must remain in it to gain points. The first player to 150 points wins. Infinite respawns; each player is on his or her own. |
| Solo Objective | Escort | Players gain points for escorting an armed officer. The first player to 50 points wins. Infinite respawns; each player is on his or her own. |
| | Flag Carry | Pick up the flag for points. The flag drops when you are killed. The one with the most points when time is up wins. Infinite respawns; each player is on his or her own. |

# The Drone

One unique asset you have available during co-op and team missions in *Ghost Recon: Advance Warfighter 2* is the drone, an automated recon vessel that is able to silently hover above the map and scan the horizon for enemy activity, then relay the position of enemies back to the Ghosts as long as the target remains in the sight of the drone's cameras. When a drone spots an enemy, it paints a red diamond on the target, and all Ghosts can then see the target on their HUD. However, the red diamond indicates only the position of the target on the HUD, not its distance from the Ghost.

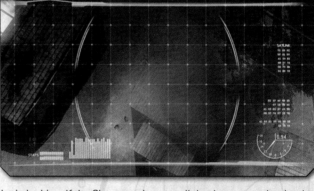

Ghosts can direct the movement of the drone from the ground. Pressing up on the D-pad activates the Drone order, which commands the drone to move in the direction the Ghost issuing the order is looking. If the Ghost needs to recall the drone to gather intel on the current position, pressing down on the D-pad issues the Call Drone command.

The drone is one of the most useful tools the Ghosts have in war games and campaigns. As such, it becomes a target to the opposition. The drone can be sniped out of the sky, instantly removing all gathered intel from the Ghost HUD. However, the drone is a small target because it hovers so high in the sky. Shoot at it only when you have a clear shot, because while looking up at it you may not detect an enemy creeping up from behind you.

# Multiplayer Tips

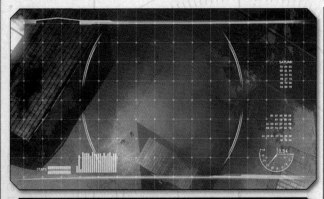

- Claymore mines are great for ambushing the enemy. Set them around corners or near cover. Remember that they explode out in the direction you are facing when you place them and can kill enemies several meters away.

- Communicate with your team during the setup phase of the mission. Ensure that you have a variety of soldier classes. A team of all marksmen will have a tough time if the enemy gets in close. While riflemen are the most versatile, it is a good idea to have at least one of each of the other classes as well.

- Always seek the high ground. Many of the maps have hills or buildings where you can access the roof or upper story. When possible, use these elevated positions to fire down on your opponents.

- Take the time to move from one piece of cover to the next while teammates provide cover. Never stray too far out of your teammates' line of sight—if they can't see you, they can't support you.

- Defenders should avoid camping on their main objective, as organized assaults from multiple directions are difficult to survive. It's better to spread out and intercept attackers en route to the objective, where they're less prepared to face resistance.

- When on a team, be careful not to bunch up. Not only are you easier to detect as a group, but a well-placed grenade could take out several of you at once.

- Use the tactical map to coordinate your teams' actions.

- When firing at medium to long range, either use semi-automatic or burst fire mode. If your weapon has only full auto, keep your fire down to short bursts.

- Determine the enemy's main routes of advance during Defend missions and set up ambushes at right angles to their advance to catch them in ambushes from the flanks.

- Though you can move into cover as in the single-player campaign, stay behind objects that will block the enemy's fire.

- For solo missions, Rifleman class is best since it allows you to deal with a variety of circumstances.

- Look for choke points—narrow areas on a map that limit movement—and set or watch for ambushes in such areas.

- Grenades work great in enclosed areas where walls and other objects will keep them near your target.

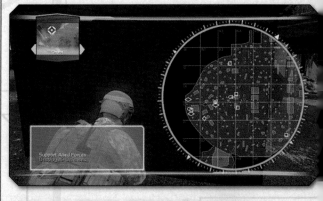

# The Maps

*Ghost Recon Advanced Warfighter 2* includes 18 maps for your multiplayer pleasure. Some of these maps offer two settings for lighting—allowing you to play them in daylight and either low light or night.

## AFTERMATH

This flooded city features debris and deluged cars throughout the streets, offering cover for both sides. Buildings in the center of town all have balconies and high stone walls, making long-range engagements and close-quarter fights both viable choices. This map can be played on both day and night lighting settings and is suitable for 8–12 players.

## BACK ALLEY

A small urban town positioned around a bridge running through the middle of the city is the setting. Multiple alleyways and paths allow for a tactical choice of moving in from above or below the enemy. Lighting can be set at day or sunset, and the map is suitable for 8–12 players.

# CALDERA

This massive construction site has the foundation for a large satellite dish built in the center. Moving into the interior of the dish can be tricky, since it lends itself to very close-quarter battles, while the elevated northern part of the map offers some long sight lines. Battle on this map take place during the day, and the map is suitable for 12–16 players.

# CRASH SITE

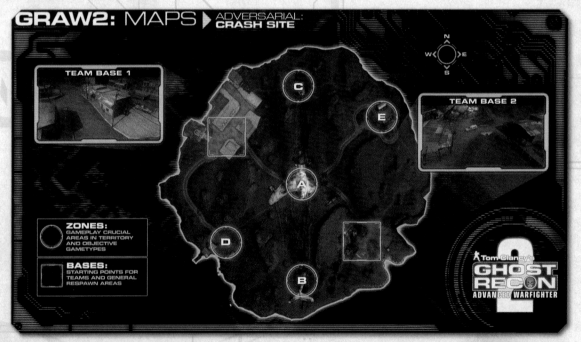

This map is a large open valley with a half-mile-long trench dug into the middle of it by a downed airplane. Hills in the area offer long sight lines, while debris from the wreck provides plenty of cover. Lighting options are midday and morning haze, and the map is suitable for 12–16 players.

# EMBASSY

Open city streets lead to a large embassy building near the shores. The embassy's roof provides an excellent sniper point, and there are plenty of back alleys to afford a more tactical approach. This map can be played in day or sunset lighting and is suitable for 8—12 players.

# FORT

A disused historical fort looks over the sea, with lush vegetation all around its base. The jungle around the base provides cover as you move up to the fort itself. This map can be played both day and night and is suitable for 8—12 players.

# HEADQUARTERS

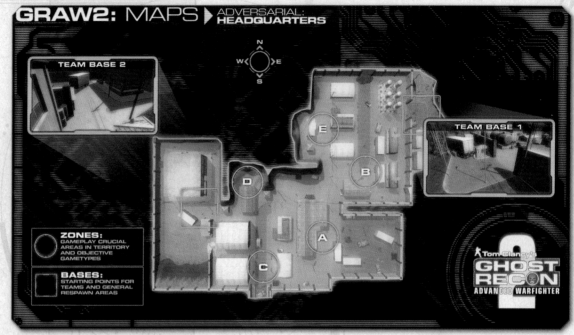

This command and control facility features various warehouses and other buildings recently used by a local militia. Two buildings are [...] have guard posts on top, allowing for excellent firing positions, while the rest of the layout is set up for much closer combat. Combat ta[...] place during the day, and the map is suitable for 4–8 players.

# HIDEOUT

An evacuated village with a church is the center of conflict in this area. The deserted streets in the town lend themselves to midrange [...] combat, while a rocky valley nearby offers up some close-quarter engagements. Day is the only lighting option, and the map is suitable for 8–12 players.

# HYDRODAM

This large hydroelectric dam sits on the side of a lake. Long sight lines offer great sniper support for both sides, and paths underground give each team the chance to infiltrate the other base undetected. This map can be played on day or sunrise settings and is suitable for 12–16 players.

# LAGOON

A beautiful rocky island features crystal-clear waters and a shipwreck at the center of the lagoon. Large boulders lend themselves to great cover points, and the vegetation throughout the forested areas also offers excellent camouflage. Lighting can be either day or evening, and the map is suitable for 12–16 players.

# LOCKS

A pinnacle of human engineering, the locks were built to raise and lower ships passing through the canal to the appropriate sea level needed to continue their course. Long sight lines across the entire map make this area a sniper's dream. Battle takes place during the day, and the map is suitable for 12–16 players.

# MONUMENT HILL

An urban town built on a hill, Monument Hill features open streets and alleyways leading up to a marketplace. The alleys offer protectio[n] from an advance on the center, while balconies on opposite sides of the plaza give snipers excellent lines of sight. This map can be play[ed] with daytime or overcast lighting and is suitable for 12–16 players.

# OUTPOST

A main outpost, this map features one central building filled with disused factory equipment; the building is surrounded by smaller warehouses. The whole area is quite open, so mid- to long-range encounters are to be expected. Daytime lighting is the only option, and the map is suitable for 8–12 players.

# PIPELINE

A large rusted pipe elevated above the ground winds its way down from the outpost. Three small encampments offer some cover, and a bridge over the pipeline is an excellent elevated position for marksmen to test their skill. This map is set during the day and is suitable for 4–8 players.

# RIVERBANK

Rocky cliffs cut out from the initial excavation of the cut, have isolated this base on the side of the canyon. Open-air buildings filled with various crates and shipments offer excellent protection while you advance on the enemy. This map is set for daytime lighting and is suitable for 4–8 players.

# SHORELINE

A village is situated between a sprawling beachfront and the canal's locks. High walls and long sight lines offer up many chances for intense firefights. Daytime is the sole lighting option, and the map is suitable for 4–8 players.

# STATION

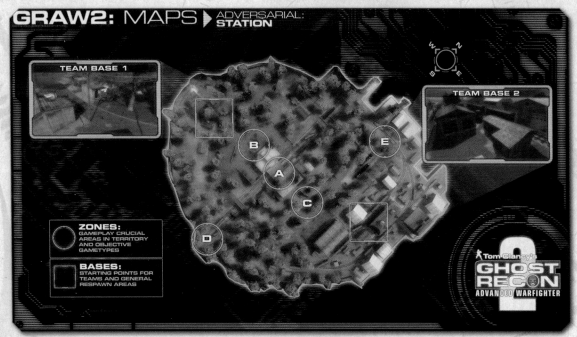

A devastated railway is cluttered with run-down train cars at both the station and train yard nearby. Terrain around the station offers cover up to the center, where the action switches to close-range engagements throughout the buildings. The lighting is daytime, and the map is suitable for 12–16 players.

# THE CUT

Excavated rock and dirt at the side of the cut offer up an excellent position for this encampment and facility. High cliffs provide excellent snipe positions, and the dense vegetation also provides cover for tactical maneuvers. This map is set during the day and is suitable for 8–12 players.

## SINGLE-PLAYER ACHIEVEMENTS

| Achievement | Requirement | Gamer Score Points |
|---|---|---|
| Challenge 1 Complete | You have mastered the first challenge in the tutorial. | 10 |
| Challenge 2 Complete | You have mastered the second challenge in the tutorial. | 10 |
| Challenge 3 Complete | You have mastered the third challenge in the tutorial. | 10 |
| Challenge 4 Complete | You have mastered the fourth challenge in the tutorial. | 10 |
| Tutorial Walkthrough | You went through the whole tutorial. | 5 |
| Act 1 (Missions 1–3) Complete (Low Risk) | You have completed Act 1 in low risk. | 10 |
| Act 2 Complete (Missions 4–10) (Low Risk) | You have completed Act 2 in low risk. | 15 |
| Act 3 Complete (Missions 11–12) (Low Risk) | You have completed Act 3 in low risk. | 20 |
| Act 1 Complete (Guarded Risk) | You have completed Act 1 in guarded risk. | 20 |
| Act 2 Complete (Guarded Risk) | You have completed Act 2 in guarded risk. | 25 |
| Act 3 Complete (Guarded Risk) | You have completed Act 3 in guarded risk. | 30 |
| Act 1 Complete (Elevated Risk) | You have completed Act 1 in elevated risk. | 30 |
| Act 2 Complete (Elevated Risk) | You have completed Act 2 in elevated risk. | 35 |
| Act 3 Complete (Elevated Risk) | You have completed Act 3 in elevated risk. | 40 |
| Bull's Eye (Quick Mission) | Finish a mission with a 100% accuracy statistic. | 30 |
| Hawk's Eye (Quick Mission) | You have finished a mission with all of your intel markers acquired while out of combat. | 30 |
| Iron Man (Quick Mission) | You have finished a mission without being hit. | 30 |
| Predator (Quick Mission) | You have finished a mission with all fights engaged by you. | 30 |

| Achievement | Requirement | Gamer Score Points |
|---|---|---|
| Team ELITE (Quick Mission) | You have finished a mission with an ace team. | 30 |
| Mission Accomplished | Complete all the secondary objectives in Campaign mode or in Quick Mission mode. | 30 |
| Single Player Master | Unlock all other single-player mode achievements. | 50 |

## MULTIPLAYER ACHIEVEMENTS

| Achievement | Requirement | Gamer Score Points |
|---|---|---|
| Team Veteran | Win 30 team matches with at least 5 gamertags in the room. | 25 |
| Solo Veteran | Win 10 solo matches with at least 5 gamertags in the room. | 25 |
| Co-op Veteran | Win 30 co-op matches with at least 5 gamertags in the room. | 25 |
| Ultimate Defender | Win a 60-minute co-op Defend match on any map. | 40 |
| Helo Hunter | Shoot down 20 helicopters in the Helicopter Hunt game type. | 20 |
| Demo Expert | Plant 10 demo charges in Team Mission matches with at least 5 gamertags in the room. | 20 |
| Combat Medic | Heal 10 teammates wounded by enemy fire in a multiplayer match with at least 5 gamertags in the room. | 25 |
| Team MVP | Lead your team in kills in a team match with at least 5 gamertags on your team. | 15 |
| Team All-Star | Lead your team in kills in 10 team matches with at least 5 gamertags on your team. | 35 |
| Enforcer | Eliminate 5 different human opponents in 30 seconds with at least 10 gamertags in the room. | 20 |
| Threatening | Get a total of 50 kills in team or solo matches with at least 5 gamertags in the room. | 10 |
| Dangerous | Get a total of 150 kills in team or solo matches with at least 5 gamertags in the room. | 15 |
| Lethal | Get a total of 300 kills in team or solo matches with at least 5 gamertags in the room. | 20 |
| Ruthless | Get a total of 500 kills in team or solo matches with at least 5 gamertags in the room. | 25 |
| Sniper Expert | Get a total of 100 sniper rifle kills in team or solo matches with at least 5 gamertags in the room. | 20 |
| Station (Co-op 1) Perfect | Complete co-op campaign mission without failing an objective, with no respawns, on default or hard. | 20 |
| The Cut (Co-op 2) Perfect | Complete co-op campaign mission without failing an objective, with no respawns, on default or hard. | 20 |

| Achievement | Requirement | Gamer Score Points |
|---|---|---|
| Locks (Co-op 3) Perfect | Complete co-op campaign mission without failing an objective, with no respawns, on default or hard. | 20 |
| Caldera (Co-op 4) Perfect | Complete co-op campaign mission without failing an objective, with no respawns, on default or hard. | 20 |
| Outpost (Co-op 5) Perfect | Complete co-op campaign mission without failing an objective, with no respawns, on default or hard. | 20 |
| Hideout (Co-op 6) Perfect | Complete co-op campaign mission without failing an objective, with no respawns, on default or hard. | 20 |
| Perfect Co-op Campaign | Complete all co-op campaign missions without failing an objective, with no respawns, on default or hard. | 40 |

XBOX 360 ACHIEVEMENTS